How To FSBO Your Home And Do A Better Job Than an Agent

FSBO Power Tips And Tools

---

1 in 8 Homes Is Sold Direct

Study Shows A Home Is Shown On Average Only 8 Times Before It Sells!

About the Author

It's your money. Don't give it away!

Sissy Lappin has more than 25 years of experience in real estate sales. With *Simple and SOLD*, she shares her personal knowledge and teaches you how to sell your house without paying an exorbitant broker's commission.

The best insider tips, cost–effective Internet strategies, and secret real estate industry tactics are all in this book. Read it before you even think about calling a real estate agent!

Simple and SOLD takes you through the process step–by–step. It is an invaluable, indispensable, easy–to–use GUIDE and the only tool you'll need to sell your home and avoid paying broker fees. You keep your money in your own pocket.

Full disclosure: after the 1st edition and readers requests, Sissy co–founded ListingDoor.com—a one stop professional set of tools to price, list, market, and sell your own home without hiring and paying an agent.

Simple and SOLD™

SELL YOUR HOME FAST AND KEEP THE COMMISSION #1 FSBO GUIDE:

Selling Your House For Sale By Owner & Save Money!

SISSY LAPPIN

Founder, ListingDoor

LAUNCHED Publishing

Published by

LAUNCHED Publishing

Second Edition 2.21

Trade Paperback ISBN: 978-0-9849283-9-2
Ebook ISBN: 978-0-9884168-5-7
Library of Congress Control Number: 2011962624

Publishers Cataloging-in-Publication Data

Lappin, Sissy.

Simple and *SOLD* – Sell Your Home Fast and Keep the Commission #1 FSBO Guide

/ Sissy Lappin. — 2nd Ed. — Houston, TX : LAUNCHED Publishing, c2017.

p. ; cm.

ISBN: 978-0-9849283-9-2 (pbk.) ; 978-0-9884168-5-7 (ebk.)

At head of title: Sell your Home Fast and Keep the Commission #1 FSBO Guide

Summary: Simple and *SOLD* gives you the proven tools and effective strategies used by the best real estate insiders to sell your home FSBO. Sissy walks you through the step-by-step process from start to finish to price, list, market and sell your home without hiring and paying a real estate agent....confidence included! — Publisher.

1. Home selling--United States--Handbooks, manuals, etc. 2. Home selling--United States--Computer network resources--Handbooks, manuals, etc. 3. Short selling--United States--Handbooks, manuals, etc. 4. Internet marketing. 5. Real estate business--United States--Marketing--Handbooks, manuals, etc. 6. Vendors and purchasers--United States--Handbooks, manuals, etc. I. Title.

HD259 .L36 2012 2011962624

643/.120973--dc23 1203

Printed in the United States of America, on acid-free paper.

Book and jacket design: Patricia Bacall

CONTENTS

ACKNOWLEDGEMENTS

A very special thank you to Jia Tolentino, who shaped my thoughts into what you see on the page and without whom this book would never have come to life.

I also want to thank my amazing clients from the last 25 years, many of whom have become my friends. Thank you for urging me to share my knowledge with the public, "just in case I got hit by a bus." Working with all of you is the reason I wrote *Simple and SOLD.*

Then there are the entrepreneurs and social thinkers whose thoughts inspired me to start this book and I want to thank them, too. Some of them I know, some I do not, but all of them bring power and a voice to the American consumer and entrepreneur. If you happen to be curious, please go to SissyLappin.com [http://po.st/simplesold18] where I have elaborated on the amazing messages put forth by each of them.

Tony Hsieh
Jason Fried and David Heinemeier Hansson
Malcolm Gladwell
Steven Levitt and Stephen Dubner
Jim Trippon
Keith Cunningham
My Family

THE REAL COMMISSION RATE

THE REAL ESTATE COMMISSION IS NOT 6%. FOR MOST HOMEOWNERS IT'S 40–60% OF THEIR HOME'S EQUITY!

Let's say your house is worth $400,000 and your equity is $60,000. You hire a real estate agent who charges the customary 6% commission. Even if your home sells for its full value, you'll end up paying the agent $24,000. There goes 40% of your equity. You've lost a significant chunk of real, hard cash that cannot be recouped.

$ 400,000	house sale price
$ −340,000	mortgage
$ 60,000	equity
$ −24,000	6% real estate commission fee
$ 36,000	equity remaining
= 40%	of your equity gone

★★ A 40% true commission rate! ★★

Discover your true cost with ListingDoor equity calculator. [http://po.st/simplesold19]

Your home equity is like your 401(k): it's a financial Holy Grail. For Unless it's a matter of life or death or putting food on the table, don't touch either.

You might be thinking that you have no choice. That's how the system works. That's what you have to do when you sell a home, right?

Wrong! *Simple and SOLD* shows you that you have a choice and spells that choice out for you, step–by–step. Keep reading.

READ THIS FIRST

The purpose of this book is to enable homeowners to rock at selling their own homes. We assume you have never sold a home before and have no knowledge of the process. What you'll learn here is how simple the process is, especially when it is broken down into easy–to–follow steps. We know how a commission takes on a whole new meaning when seen through a seller's eyes.

Simple and SOLD is based on knowledge, not theory. We wanted to give homeowners a diligently prepared and legitimate alternative so they can choose what's best for their personal situation.

There are two versions of this book: digital and print. The digital version has hyperlinks (underlined in the print version) that you can click for added convenience. The print version has the short URLs. Yes, some of the hyperlinks link back to *ListingDoor.com* but there's no bait–and–switch here. We developed *ListingDoor.com* to make selling your own home even simpler. If you are a visual learner, like myself, it makes it easier. The goal of both *Simple and SOLD* and *ListingDoor.com* is to educate you on how to easily sell your own home and make the process fun, fast, and professional. Confidence included.

FOREWORD

Kathy's voice sounded desperate. "I need you to come over," she said. "I don't know what to do anymore."

My friend's financial situation was out of control. Her ex-husband had failed to come through with the monthly child support, and she wasn't able to make the house payment—again.

If you've never been late with a mortgage payment, you don't know what stress is. The four walls that protect you—the very roof over your children's heads—is in jeopardy. It's terrifying.

It's also humiliating. With websites like RealtyTrac [http://po.st/simplesold34], your neighbors can tell if you are one day late with that payment—and if you head into foreclosure, the whole world will know.

I knew my friend hadn't meant to let her finances get so bad. She is one of the most amazing people I know.

But sometimes people find themselves in situations where they feel powerless, and that can create fear that's paralyzing. By not taking action, she let things get worse.

Kathy is a smart, capable lady. She was just scared; that's all.

Her home had become more of a financial burden than she could bear, and she knew that selling it would help ease the strain. If she could sell it at market price, she might make a little bit more than she still owed on the mortgage—enough profit to help her and the kids start over in a new place.

"But I'm not sure I'd even make enough profit to cover the real estate agent's commission," she said miserably. "I feel so trapped."

"What if you could sell it without an agent?" I asked.

Kathy laughed sadly. "I have a full–time job. I don't have time to go to real estate school."

"Maybe you don't have to," I said.

I drove to my friend's house that night determined to help her. As we sat sipping our way through a second cup of coffee, I realized that Kathy was under a misconception. She believed that selling a house was extremely complicated and difficult—in fact, she felt it was something she could not do herself.

Well, that night, she learned how. We went over the steps to making a successful house sale, and before dawn—actually, I think I drove home around 12:30 a.m.—Kathy seemed like a different person.

And she was different. She was empowered. I helped her realize that when you take something one step at a time, it's possible. It's often not even as difficult as you thought!

Kathy saved her credit rating by learning how to do something she thought she could never do: she sold her house.

Can you picture yourself in her shoes—or are you in those shoes at this very moment? Do you need to sell your house, but you think it's something only a person with many years of training and expertise could handle?

Do you feel you'd be lost about where to even start, and not confident enough to manage the pricing, the negotiating, and the closing?

A single mother with three kids did it. Thousands and thousands of people have done it.

Whatever your reason—you can do it, too. It's just not hard.

INTRODUCTION

I wish I could brag and say I was an engineer at NASA before my real estate career, but the only real job I had before real estate was gift wrapping at Neiman Marcus!

I was a girl fresh out of college the first time I tried to get a job in real estate. I headed straight for one of Houston's largest residential brokerage firms and applied with confidence.

I did just fine in the interview, but when it came to the written personality test—well, I distinctly remember the personnel lady walking over to me while I was waiting in the lobby and blurting out, "Honey, you're never going to work in real estate."

So I put that dream on hold and worked in odd jobs for a few years. But at the age of twenty–five, something happened that would change my life: I experienced my first foreclosure.

I had made the huge mistake of co–signing on a house with a family member who let payments lapse. Before I knew it, I was entangled in a massive financial mess. But that foreclosure taught me a lesson.

After thinking about it for almost three decades, I came to a startling conclusion: if I had handled the sale myself and not had to pay the 6 percent commission to the real estate agent, I could have saved my house.

Right around the time that I was dealing with that foreclosure, I met a man in Austin, Texas who got me back into the real estate business. His name was Rod G. When I told him the story of my early and failed attempts to take the world of real estate by storm, he shrugged it off.

"In this business, real estate agents mess things up more than they facilitate anything," he told me. "I like the fact that you have no experience. I like the way you approach things and the perspective you have." He hired me, and I've never looked back.

Today, I've marketed over half a billion dollars in real estate—and I can humbly acknowledge that Mr. Gordy was right to believe in me. And if someone who bombed her first personality test could become successful in this field, anyone can.

The Internet's doing the work, so why do things seem the same?

Maybe your grandparents and parents had real estate agents handle their home sales. But that was before the advent of the amazing Internet.

With the Internet, buyers and sellers can find each other easily and directly. All the information you need to sell a home is available online, too—although this book will save you many hours of sifting through web pages to get that information.

When an agent sells your home, you are a spectator in the process. By selling your home yourself, using this book and online resources, you will be in charge of the process—and that's a great feeling!

In your hands, your home sale will be personal, which gives you a competitive edge. Knowing how to sell a house will also become a powerful tool in your possession. From now on, every time you or someone in your family buys or sells a house, you'll have the practical business expertise to carry out the transaction yourself. Since the average American moves every five years, that skill can save you and your loved ones a great deal of hard, tangible cash.

Why don't real estate agents use the Internet to market houses? Most of them simply use the Multiple Listing Service (MLS), because it is the system that has been used for years. Yet, three of the top four real estate listing sites are Zillow, Trulia, and Yahoo! Real Estate, according to Experian's Hitwise monitoring service.

For years, I have expected real estate firms to reinvent themselves and change to a business model that's more modern and fair to the consumer. But that hasn't happened.

Most agencies have never adopted new technology, even though they've seen thousands of homes being sold without the help of agents. They've also watched thousands of homeowners lose their homes to foreclosure, including homes that might have been saved if the agents were willing to reduce their commissions.

It's notable that states with the highest number of foreclosures also have the highest real estate agent commission rates.

Real estate myth-busting

Myth # 1 — Homes that are sold with a real estate agent sell for more money.

Fact: *Two independent studies show the complete opposite. Stanford and Northwestern University concluded from their studies that homes sold without an agent sold for an average of 4-7% higher when no agent was involved. The only study that shows this is the one by the National Association of REALTORS® (NAR) — 100% funded by Realtors®*

Myth # 2 — Everyone uses a real estate agent and pays a commission.

Fact: *According to National Association of REALTORS (NAR) Profile of Buyers and Sellers, the number of full-service commissions fell from 24 percent in 2011 to 21 percent in 2012. In 2013, the number was below 20 percent. In order for brokerages to secure their future, they're going to have to make some adjustments. Both buyers and sellers are becoming extremely commission-sensitive.*

Myth # 3 — The agent's commission is only 5–6% of the home.

Fact: *This 5-6% is misleading. Comparing the percentage of the agent's commission to your home's equity is a more accurate way of showing costs. The commission you pay your agent for most sellers is 40-60% of your equity. According to the NAR, Americans don't earn 6% equity in their home until they've owned it for 8 to10 years. A study conducted by Georgia Institute of Technology showed that it takes 2 to 5 years to recoup even a 4% loss.*

Houses sell faster and for more money in a good market. In a bad market, it takes longer and houses sell for less. But they do sell in both kinds of markets.

Why put 6 to 8 percent or more of your home's value into the pocket of an agent? Remember, you'll owe that commission even if you only break even on the house. In other words, if you use an agent, your house sale might put you further into debt instead of making you any profit.

Maybe you think house sales are faster when you use an agent, or that the agent will help you through the emotional aspects of selling your home. Unfortunately, neither is true.

Your house will sell quickly when you find the right buyer. You're far more motivated to find that buyer than your agent is. The agent isn't there to counsel you; he or she is there to make a commission. The agent will naturally put the most time into properties that will make them the biggest commission—and if your house isn't the most marketable or most expensive one they're handling, you might be out of luck.

Now, more than ever, you can and should be able to sell your house without having to pay a commission—by selling it yourself.

Just by picking up this book, you've started the process of gathering the information you need. You can use Internet–enabled market awareness to work for you—no matter which way you choose. *Simple and SOLD* gives practical advice based on experience, not theory.

Can you really do this yourself?

I've written this book for people with absolutely no experience. There is no mystique in what a real estate agent does; the only requirement is common sense. Consider me a voice of reason, a friend with more than two decades as a specialist in the real estate market talking to you through this little book and helping you discover a way to take charge.

And if you're daunted by the idea of essentially learning a new business just for one transaction, let me remind you: 6 percent of the value of your home is *a ton of money.* If you think of the bite that the commission will take out of your home equity, it might seem like two tons of money.

Will it take you months or years to learn how to sell your house? Take a look at the size of the book you're holding. As much as I would like to have written a thick, impressive encyclopedia of wisdom, you don't need that. This book is exactly the information you need to sell your home yourself.

You're reading this because you want to learn about selling your own home. If you're not a real estate professional (although you'll find out in the next chapter that it doesn't take much to call yourself a professional in this field), and you haven't had the chance to make your own blunders, you'll learn from my mistakes to avoid making any of your own.

Take my experience for all it can give you. I've learned how to cut the nonsense out of my real estate deals and save my clients money. I've learned how to sell houses with measurable, reliable, superior results—and now I want to teach you!

Independence Day

This is a crucial fact to understand: the issues involved in selling a home are the same, no matter the price point. Although I live and work in Houston, I've closed huge deals all over the country and consulted all over the country. I've sold homes from five to eight figures in value, and the same problems and solutions came up every time. The stories in this book are true, and they teach you fundamental truths about the business of real estate.

And the reason why I'm so sure that you can sell your own home is that, for 20 of my years in real estate, I've been working as an independent agent.

I started my real estate career at a big firm, but I quickly realized I could not be happy with the inefficiency I saw there. I wanted to work—but it seemed to me the agents accomplished little while creating "busy work" so they could justify their commissions.

Real estate firms are known for their flamboyance. The brands in the parking lot are Mercedes, BMW, occasionally even Rolls Royce—and they're always in the society section of the newspaper. You get the picture.

Most of the heads of these firms are rich, but they're also out of touch with current reality. Many of them have not sold a home since the Internet was invented!

These same executives all said I would fail as a one-woman operation because I could not compete with "the big boys." They called me unprofessional because I didn't have a store-front office. Now they are all trying to negotiate out of their office space leases and rent smaller spaces because so much real estate business today is done at the local Starbucks. I guess my approach no longer seems so unprofessional!

They might call my success a "fluke," but it is a very long fluke.

Once I started making big money, these same agency owners would invite me to lunch and let me know that if I ever wanted to come on board, I would be welcome. They began to offer me assistants and a higher commission split, so I could "travel"—and I guess then I'd be in the society pages, too!

These executives have a hard time understanding how a single person could outperform their top producers without spending wildly. Yet, I am doing just that.

They still live in the world where you need to have an advertising department for newspaper ads, sales meetings and managers, an appointment desk, and lots of unused office space in order to sell houses. This antiquated business model works for them, but they are charging their customers for it—and the customer does not have a choice.

I believe competition is for the competent, and it is time to give real estate agencies some real competition.

I work for myself and by myself, and it's taught me that working alone is truly the best way to streamline this process down to the essentials while never forgetting a detail.

As a person who wants to buy or sell a home, *you* don't have a real estate office with a receptionist to make appointments, do you? Well, neither do I. If I can sell homes with my laptop, you can see how unimportant the real estate office really is.

The perks of being a one–woman show are unending. For one, I make a lot more money than other real estate agents because I don't have to pay for assistants and a bunch of assorted staffs. Best of all, working on my own allows me to deal with people directly, which makes this business a lot easier and more efficient.

I can't tell you how many times I've been on the phone with another real estate agent and wanted to scream, "Can I please just talk to your client?" It's so much easier when you're dealing directly with the people who make the decisions.

> **FACT:** *the issues involved in selling a home are the same, no matter the price point with which you're working. I sell homes from 5 to 8 figures, and the same problems and solutions come up every time.*

I once had a $9.4 million deal that was about to fail because the buyer and seller were $200,000 apart, and neither wanted to budge. In an unorthodox move, I asked the listing agent if I could call the seller (a famous basketball player) directly.

When I got the guy on the phone, I asked him what I could do to keep this deal from falling through—and I kept him chatting for a little bit. During our conversation, it came up that he and his friends were still looking for a place to stay in San Diego during the Super Bowl.

"That whole town is booked up solid," he complained.

"Well, I happen to know someone who has an empty condo in San Diego," I said, "and it's the guy who wants to buy your house."

"Are you serious?"

"I am. So I have an idea. Would you come down $100,000 on the price of your house if the buyer comes up $100,000—and throws in his San Diego place for the weekend?"

The deal was closed within minutes. In fact, the buyer and seller are now friends.

You might not be selling a multi-million dollar home—your ace might be something like the barbecue pit in the backyard—but the same principles apply. Talking directly to the person making the buying decisions can make all the difference when you sell your house. Only you know all the details that might make the deal work.

I'm one of the largest independent agents in the country, and that's how I work. My success should show you that cutting out all the nonsense and dealing person-to-person is absolutely the key to buying and selling homes.

My clients have all been satisfied. Here's how I can tell. Typically, about 20 percent of clients refer their friends and colleagues to their real estate agent—but 90 percent of my clients do.

The problem with real estate books

Many of the real estate books on the market today belong in the fiction section. They may have the words "How to Sell Your Home" in the title, but most of these books should be called "How to Stage Your Home." While home staging—making your house look pretty and valuable—is important, anyone in the industry knows that staging is *not* the engine that drives home sales.

The other group of real estate books are the "get rich quick" infomercial types, full of flashy promises but short on useful information. I designed this book to be a useful textbook for the average homeowner who wants or needs to sell a house and wants to have the skill to sell a house whenever the need arises.

You already know that you'll need to fix and clean and paint and generally doll up your house in order to get buyers interested. But you might not know how to handle real estate negotiations and what to expect at each step of the sales process. That's what I'm here to teach you.

FACT: *This book isn't a sales pitch; it's advice from one independent seller to another.*

There are websites that will give you some of this information, but what you read might not be complete—or even completely trustworthy. That's why I wrote a book that will warn you about the possible pitfalls of selling your home and explain why you need to take each of the steps you'll take.

I've written my book primarily for people with no real estate experience, because you won't need it—you'll just need a good dose of common sense. I also wrote it short and straight to the point. I'm a working mother who knows the value of efficient time management, so you won't find a single word in this book that's going to waste your time.

Some real estate books were written by people with experience only in a booming market. I started my career during a big recession, and I know how to sell a home during a recession and during a boom.

This book also might be a useful tool for real estate agents with only a few years' experience, especially if they haven't yet worked in a recession. This isn't stuff you'll get in the little courses that you have to take before you get or renew your license. This is information that comes straight from my experience and from the advice of a dozen other real estate agents whose brains I picked about the current state of the industry.

When your agent isn't returning your calls anymore

Selling your house is a very personal matter. You are much better off handling it personally.

One of the many advantages of doing it yourself includes getting to keep the 6 to 8 percent real estate agent's commission. But to do that, you're going to have to start thinking like a specialist.

Many homeowners get caught up in their emotional attachments when it's time to sell. Our homes suddenly seem less like an asset and more like our nest, our safe place, our "take–your–shoes–off–and–have–a–cold–beer" spot.

But when you sell your own home, you have to look at your property as an investment and look at your local market for the particular realities that will affect your sale. This is not about how much you loved living in your home—it's about how much money you can get for it.

Maybe you've already tried listing your house with an agent, and it's been sitting on the market for a while—and that agent isn't calling as much as she did during those early months. That's OK. You can start where you are and take charge of the situation.

Step–by–step, this book will teach you how to understand and use those market realities as well as (if not better than) the top real estate companies in the nation.

My website is called ListingDoor.com, and it's simple. But that doesn't mean you can sell your house in five or ten minutes. It will require a little bit of time and work on your part. But the money you save on a real estate agent's commission could mean you're earning hundreds or thousands of dollars per hour for the time you put into selling it yourself. Those aren't bad wages!

Working with the big boys

I know you've got questions. We'll be devoting many parts of this book to your questions and comments, so I can respond to them even before you ask!

If you've heard of the most popular real estate listing websites—Zillow, Trulia, and Yahoo! Real Estate—you're wondering now if you are qualified to compete with home sellers on those huge sites.

The answer is: you won't be competing. In fact, you'll use those websites as assets to sell your home. I'll show you how.

FACT: *Zillow is the #1 site for home searches.*

Zillow is the biggest of the big boys—the busiest real estate site on the Internet, according to Experian's Hitwise monitoring service. It's far bigger than the MLS. You will be leveraging the strength of Zillow and other top sites to sell your house.

> *"The Web is the national MLS already. It's happened. You're arguing over yesterday's news."*
>
> – RICH BARTON, founder Zillow

These big sites will give your house exposure, and they'll be a huge asset for you—but they are all missing an important part of the equation. To sell your house the fastest and for the most money, you need a marketing plan that is specific to you, your market, and your particular home. Once you have created a plan that fits your situation, you can use these sites as strong marketing tools.

I'm here to help you create that marketing plan and to shepherd you through the process of advertising your house for sale, dealing with potential buyers, and closing the deal.

The Internet has blown apart the old rules of pretty much every industry and allowed for many new, fresh possibilities. Instead of the obsolete real estate business model, it's time now for a strategy that will bring home selling into today's world.

The best professionals keep things simple. That's what I do, and that's what you're going to do.

Your next question might be something along the lines of, "What if I'm not the kind of person who can sell stuff? What if I didn't get the salesperson gene?" As someone who has trained and mentored dozens of real estate agents, let me assure you that you *can* do this, regardless of who you are. As you'll recall, I was once told I had the wrong personality for real estate, too!

There is only one characteristic you must have to sell your house: common sense. That's it.

No one knows your home better than you. You have that unique asset going for you, and your insights about your home will come through when you are marketing it and meeting with buyers. I want this book to be the gas for your engine. By the time you're done reading it, you will feel like one of the big boys.

Simple and *SOLD*, designed for you

To see what your home-selling process will look like in action, you can turn to the website *ListingDoor.com*. I created this comprehensive, simple, virtual marketplace to give people literally everything they need to sell their own homes. It is consumer-driven technology.

This book will teach you how to sell your own home and *ListingDoor.com* provides the tools to price, list, market, and sell your own home without hiring and paying a real estate agent 10's of thousands of dollars. *ListingDoor.com* is a world-class site, and it's the first of its kind in the real estate industry. The site was designed to be all about you, your home, and your home-selling transactions.

I spent three years writing this book and creating this website after the first edition because I believe passionately that anyone, with the right knowledge and tools, can do a great job selling a home—even if they're not a real estate agent.

I listened to homeowners and took their comments to heart. I'm committed to consumer interests and a direct, personal approach because I believe that's where this industry needs to be.

Consider this: most real estate transactions fall apart because of less than a 5 percent margin. The buyer can't or won't come up with that 5 percent, and the seller can't afford to take less. That margin is less than the price of an agent's commission.

With the knowledge from this book, you'll have that amount of money as bargaining power. By not having to pay an agent, you'll be giving yourself that margin with which to work.

How to use this book

I've organized this book chronologically, using the thoughts that are probably going to go through your head. It starts with your decision to sell—or if you've already had your house on the market, with your decision to take charge of the process. Then the book walks you through selling your home, from setting the price to showing your house to negotiating the contracts, and on through the closing and into the rest of your life. Additionally I created the Simple and SOLD "Companion Workbook" for this book which is a chapter by chapter follow along highlighting the key points/must knows, tips and tricks, checklists and worksheets...all printable for quick referencing. It's free and is extremely helpful.

"Companion Workbook" Download Link
http://po.st/workbook22

FACT: *All the stories in this book are true.*

Chapter 1 gets to the first things first: in other words, why you might decide to sell and how you can decide if the time is right. We'll talk about finances, foreclosures, and situations that might make it advantageous for you to sell, no matter what the economy is doing.

Chapter 2 lets you decide for yourself whether you're going to be as good at selling your house as an agent would be. We'll discuss what an agent really does and how the Internet can give you all the advantages of an agent and more.

Chapter 3 helps you set your own perfect price. Equipped with the knowledge of how to evaluate your local market, you learn where to look to find concrete and accurate numbers. This chapter walks you through the process of getting an appraisal and shows you how to adjust your price to take your own timing into account.

Chapter 4 takes you through setting your price, from research to last–minute adjustments.

Chapter 5 teaches you the basics of marketing: telling a story, using vibrant words. This is one of the areas where you can really take advantage of doing things person–to–person instead of in the generic real estate agency model.

Chapter 6 picks up after a successful marketing period and teaches you how to show your house like a professional.

Chapter 7 is devoted to getting ready to open your door to potential buyers. I include a bit about staging, organizing, and other things you should do while waiting for the phone to ring.

Chapter 8 teaches you how to negotiate and counter your buyers' offers with all the confidence and sensibility of a pro. I show you how to respond to the buyer's needs without sacrificing your own, how to decide what's included in the sale, and what will be expected of you in terms of negotiating etiquette.

Chapter 9 explains the paperwork because I know that the length and complexity of a contract might seem overwhelming and boilerplate. Once you know what's in the paperwork, you'll know how to handle it. I teach you the whole financial process in terms you can understand.

Chapter 10 is about being inspected. It's an uncomfortable experience for many sellers, but if you have the right mindset you'll find this chapter an invaluable source of information to help prepare you for final negotiations.

Chapter 11 is about closing. I tell you how to avoid trouble and finish on top in this crucial and final stage of the transaction.

Chapter 12 has us reflect on how selling your own home differs from using an agent and how accomplishing it is going to make you feel.

And just like that, you'll be done.

Will you join me in changing the face of real estate, one house at a time?

Chapter 1

YOU CAN SELL YOUR HOME—AND YOU CAN SELL IT YOURSELF

"All the forces in the world are not so powerful as an idea whose time has come."

— Victor Hugo

Anita and Stewart built their dream house in a perfect neighborhood. They enjoyed chatting with their neighbors as they took their evening walks. Everyone knew each other. It was a true neighborhood.

Then their oldest son was accepted into a prestigious private school that was so far away; it might as well have been across the Great Wall of China. After eighteen months of hour–long commutes to and from school, Anita was going crazy. Either their son would have to quit school or they would have to move closer.

Anita and Stewart spent a night full of discussion and tears before deciding to list their house for sale—even though their friends and family were saying that "nobody" could sell a house during a recession.

They had to settle on a price. Anita said the house was "priceless." But Stewart, a wise CPA, looked at the prices for which other houses in the area had sold. Their house had great amenities, but he realized that the price had to be based on the square footage, so that's how he priced it. On the second day, it sold for 99 percent of their asking price.

They didn't make the profit they once thought they'd need to make on their dream home, but they did make enough to relocate. Their son stayed in the school he loved, and Anita got back ten hours of weekly commuting time.

Who can afford to buy a home these days? Who can afford to sell their home? Look at the commission. According to the National Association of REALTORS' own study, most homeowners do not have enough appreciation to cover the commission until they have owned their home for over 8 years.

The one dependable thing in today's world is the real estate agent's commission, which never seems to drop.

We once thought we could depend on our jobs, the government, and our investments. Now, we realize we can only depend on ourselves.

Why would anyone want to sell their own home?

There are many reasons to sell your own home. You may be coming around to the fact that you don't need to put tens of thousands of dollars in the pocket of a real estate agent for something you can do yourself. You may be attracted to the idea because you want to gain a little more control over such a personal transaction—or you may just want to try your hand at a different kind of business.

But here's a pretty good common denominator: you could use the money. Who couldn't?

The money you'll save by selling your home yourself isn't just a "bonus" for doing the work yourself: the fact is, selling your home yourself may save you from ending up in an ugly financial situation.

The perception in the past has been that people who FSBO (for sale by owner) are not fiscally responsible. Studies show the complete opposite. It is a smart, savvy, homeowner that realizes the value of money.

When I realized the commission was more than my annual salary, I decided to FSBO.

– Carol P.

Whatever your reason, remember that you're not the only one in that boat. This is a huge trend in today's real estate market. Get started by making the decision to handle your home sale yourself, and you'll be turning your real estate situation around in your favor—and you won't have to lose a big portion of your equity by paying it out as a commission to someone else.

Houses are still being bought and sold every day. Some people are taking a loss, some are breaking even, and some are even making a profit. You won't know what you can do until you try.

But you can be sure that you'll do better with this transaction if you don't have to pay commission to a real estate agent. Remember:

FACT: *The broker can only make you broker.*

Have you already tried to sell your home by listing it with an agent—and the listing expired without an offer? I have studied many MLS listings in a variety of price ranges, and a huge number of them expire during the listing period—the house remains unsold.

In many areas, over half the people who listed their homes with an agent—willing to pay that agent a full commission—ended up not selling at all. For one reason or another, those agents were not able to make the sale happen. An agent is by no means a guarantee of a sale. In the next chapter, we'll take a look at what agents do and don't do.

If you're in the half of people who listed your home with an agent and didn't get a sale, it is time to try selling it yourself.

Bottom Lines:

1. Savvy people FSBO.
2. You'll come out of the deal better if you don't have to pay a commission—especially when you consider what percentage of your equity that commission represents.
3. If your house was listed with an agent and didn't sell, it's time to try selling it again—this time without an agent.

"Companion Workbook" Download
http://po.st/workbook22

Chapter 2

DO YOU REALLY THINK I CAN DO THIS MYSELF?

Why do people believe it's almost impossible to sell their own homes? You might come across articles that tell you that. Those articles are written by real estate agents. That's like listening to the big tobacco companies tell you that smoking can't hurt you. You have to look at the source and consider their motivation.

Many houses listed with agents fail to sell. Sure, you might also hear of someone who tried to sell his own house and failed—but, in that case, I don't think it's the homeowner's failure. After all, nobody is more motivated than the owner to make the sale work.

Homeowners who tried unsuccessfully to sell their own homes didn't have the right tools to work it. It's like having a football team with no quarterback. Add a quarterback and the game changes.

This book will encourage you to become your own quarterback in the game of selling your house. Do I really think you can do it? You bet. I think there is no one better qualified to win this game than you.

There are incredible tools available today because of the Internet. You can do just about anything online, including selling your house—all without the help of an agent. In fact, the Internet system that agents use most often—the MLS—is hopelessly behind the times.

It's ridiculous that they're using technology that is so outdated. It's a Netflix world, and the MLS system hasn't changed since the days of the VCR. While the rest of the world is using Spotify, the MLS system is using eight-track tapes. And eight-track tapes are not coming back!

Doing it yourself in a DIY world

Inertia is the only thing keeping the real estate business going in its current direction—inertia and millions of dollars of political lobbying at both the state and national levels. The National Association of REALTORS is one of the largest lobbying groups in the country. It's been called on the carpet for inflating home sales by as much as 20 percent, and it never saw the housing crisis coming!

Because so much business can now be conducted entirely online, the real estate agent's fee seems especially ridiculous. Think about it. Writing a will is also a complicated business, but does an attorney charge you 5 percent of your estate for his services? These days, you don't even have to pay an attorney to write your will. You can do it online through Legal Zoom.

The Internet has empowered the average person to do so many things we never even imagined doing a few years ago. In today's Internet-driven marketplace, we can file our taxes with TurboTax, manage our investments through E*TRADE, and plan elaborate trip itineraries through Expedia. We can even find out exactly which brand of Sauvignon Blanc Aunt Liz had for dinner through her Facebook status updates!

We no longer need a middleman to give us information or perform routine tasks for us. That's why commission-based middleman industries are changing rapidly. Many have all but disappeared.

And while the Internet has revolutionized the real estate market, the real estate industry—the NAR and all the agencies it represents—is clinging to the past.

FACT: *The Internet is the most powerful democratizer of real estate.*

The big difference between the way homes are sold today, and the way they were sold a generation ago has to do with real estate search engines designed for the consumer on sites like Zillow, Trulia and Yahoo! Real Estate. These sites offer many extras and widgets that the standard MLS does not offer, and they've given the consumer the opportunity for a great real estate search experience.

These websites have blown a hole in the myth that a buyer has to call an agent to find out about a home. Buyers now search for properties online, in the convenience of their offices and homes, without ever contacting an agency.

And while real estate agents struggle to maintain their grip on the old business model, buyers in huge numbers are leveraging technology and getting rid of the needless drain on their finances that the real estate agent commission entails.

The Internet has given ordinary people access to almost all the information available to real estate agents, so conducting real estate transactions from beginning to end should be completely within the reach of the common person.

There's paperwork involved in a real estate transaction, but most of the forms are fill–in–the–blank and boilerplate. It's really not that difficult. The language may be new to you, but I'm here to serve as your translator.

"I'd like to see a strictly FSBO (for sale by owner) world," says Douglas Gantenbein, a writer for the online business and technology magazine *Slate* (in the story "Reality Bites: Why do you still need an agent to buy a home?"). "The Internet provides a perfect forum for buyers and sellers to meet, just as eBay has transformed the marketplace for everything from lace doilies to Ford F–150s."

Look at *Simple and SOLD* as a smart, hands–off–your–commission partner in this transaction. Selling a home should not be a miserable experience that costs you thousands of dollars and forces you to do something on someone else's terms.

Simple and SOLD will help you do it on your terms. It will give you information, control, advice, help, and more. It gives you more than a traditional real estate firm.

Take a stand and break with tradition

Benjamin Franklin once wrote, "Drive thy business; let it not drive thee."

The traditional method for selling a home is a process created and driven by politicians and lobbyists. It's commission–centric instead of consumer–centric. That's a cold, hard fact.

You can't control the power of the National Association of REALTORS, and you can't control the market. But you can certainly control the method you choose to sell your home. By selling your home yourself, you're refusing to let the politics of real estate be a factor in your transaction.

You're going to learn about the market first and adapt all your strategies to the general climate of the current market, as well as the particulars of your local market. With this, you'll gain a crucial element of control.

When you sell your home without an agent, you'll attract practical–minded buyers who don't want to pay their commission, either. You may choose to deal with a buyer who has an agent, but the smartest buyers today use the Internet to find properties and know that they're doing 90 percent of the legwork with their own research anyway. I could not find a study that showed how many buyers represented themselves so I did my own and the results shocked even me. It was 1 in 5 bought a home without a real estate agent.

"According to the National Association of Expert Advisors® (NAEA), 68% of buyers are not satisfied with their real estate agent's homebuyer process. Basically, this means that approximately seven out of ten buyers are not happy with their real estate agent. Those are pretty appalling numbers."

Keep in mind that if you choose to work with a real estate agent representing a buyer, a commission will have to be paid to the agent—but you'll still save money by not having to give a commission to an agent of your own.

Selling without an agent also gives you a big, personal advantage. The real estate industry makes the whole business seem complex and expensive when really, buying or selling a home is one of the most personal transactions you can make.

FACT: *Buyers today do their research on the Internet, not with real estate agents.*

As an independent thinker and seller, you're in a perfect position to show the buyer that you're working toward the same goal. When the negotiation is between two people with reasonable needs, you can get to a sale without anyone feeling like they've been taken in.

I don't mean to imply that a buyer talking to you rather than to a real estate agent will be less demanding. Of course not. But you'd be surprised at how much of a difference personal graciousness can make.

If you show the buyer that you are indeed excited at the prospect of working together, you have a much higher likelihood of being able to negotiate your own needs into the picture.

You'll also be able to control aspects of the transaction that can make or break the deal. When you're in charge of the sale, you can control the timing of your actions and the buyer's actions to simplify the process; you can control the feedback so the buyer knows exactly why he or she *should* buy your house; and most importantly, you can arrive at a perfect market price and control the way the buyer sees this price.

But I'm going to need help with this!

Yes, you will need information and guidance if you've never sold a home before. That's why I created *ListingDoor.com*, a website with the nuts and bolts to get the job done. I made it as simple as possible to use, so you can just fill in the blanks and create a successful home sales plan. It's set up like a "paint by the numbers" project so that, if you follow the instructions and fill in the blanks, you can create your own masterpiece. I based the *ListingDoor.com* system on the same system I use every day to sell houses from my laptop.

What's an agent, anyway?

People seem to think that a real estate agent's work is incredibly complex. If you're spending lots of time on something and charging thousands of dollars for it, your job has to be difficult—right? Wrong. So much of what an agent does is wasted time.

Don't be confused by the talk: "Yes, Mr. Seller, I can help you sell your home, but here's what we need to do. We need to look at the overall sales rate and take the DOM and divide it by the actuals—units, not volume—to get an accurate absorption rate. Then I'll do a CMA on your home, and we can overlay that with the absorption rate to project possible selling time, but of course we need to factor in market attrition, too ...."

This sounds complex and confusing—impossible for the untrained homeowner to grasp. So many new words! So many abbreviations! But really, it's nothing but jargon, intended to intimidate home sellers into thinking that they need the real estate agent more than they actually do.

Once you know what's involved in selling your home, you'll realize that it's not rocket science. If you still have doubts, think about this: the average cosmetologist has more far industry education and training (usually about 1,000 hours) than the average real estate agent (usually from 150 to 200 hours of training). And honestly, while I'd never trust someone to do my hair if her only qualification was having read a book called *Doing Hair for Amateurs*, I'd do business with anyone who has read this book carefully. And my hairdresser gives much better customer service than many of the real estate agents I've met!

Let's talk about what it takes to become a real estate agent. I use Texas because Texas is one of the hardest states in which to get a license. In Texas, as in most states, the majority of the courses you need to take before receiving your license are about ethics. That's right, ethics. I never took one course in how to negotiate a contract or price a home. Real estate agents learn this process by trial and error, and someone's home is a very expensive asset on which to train.

I got most of my training in real estate by reading books about real estate cycles and about the art of negotiating. I don't know another real estate agent who has done this; I'm sure they are out there, but I haven't found them. Most agents learn by doing, and the rookie agents make plenty of mistakes.

So, becoming an agent really requires taking courses on the ethics of the real estate business and then passing an exam that never tests you on your negotiation skills or the other skills an agent will need to be successful.

You can sell a home if you know what you're dealing with and use common sense. And you can do it without using the jargon that agents use to make themselves seem like a crucial part of the process.

Will there be math involved?

Don't worry if you're confused by calculations and paperwork. The contracts you'll need are all "fill in the blank" forms provided by each state. *ListingDoor.com* provides you with consumer–friendly guides.

This book wasn't written by a Washington lobby group that is funded by real estate agents whose mission is to make the business seem complicated in order to save the agent's commission. I've used everyday terms to explain all anyone needs to understand about real estate.

Really, the primary role of the real estate agent today is to carry information between the buyer and seller. There's no reason why you can't cut out the middleman and sell your home by communicating directly. It actually makes better sense to do so, and it will be a much more pleasant experience for both you and the buyer.

Without a middleman, less information will get lost in translation. You'll also eliminate the danger of an emotional real estate agent who might be in desperate need of a paycheck and attempting to persuade you to take a low bid so the deal will be done with—all the while wearing a poker face and trying to convince you of his objectivity.

What does an agent actually do?

A lot of people don't understand what actually happens behind the wizard's curtain in real estate firms. You should know that a lot of energy and employee hours (and, following that, money) are wasted there. Take the process of making an appointment for a buyer:

1. Potential buyer calls real estate agent to set up a showing.
2. Real estate agent calls listing firm property desk to set appointment.
3. Listing firm calls homeowner to set appointment.
4. Listing firm calls agent to confirm appointment.
5. Agent calls client to confirm appointment.

That's five calls because of the middlemen! No wonder they charge that huge commission: they have to pay for that wasted time somehow! Can you imagine how many more calls there'd be if the first proposed appointment time didn't work?

Modern homebuyers and sellers don't have to make even one phone call. Appointments can be scheduled over the Internet.

Real estate brokerage firms don't make appointments over the Internet for a few reasons. As a group, they are not the most tech-savvy—and the more streamlined the process, the less necessary agents will seem.

At many brokerages, agents are required to do unpaid phone duty under the marketing premise that they might pick up a new client while scheduling appointments. This system has been in place for so long that no one's really challenged it. But it means that the person answering the agency's phone might be in a resentful and unmotivated mood because he or she is working for nothing!

I'm not here to bash real estate agents—I am one! I'm not here to bash agencies either, although I personally prefer to work in the most direct and efficient way possible. Nor am I trying to bash the traditional business model. After all, it was all a perfectly logical system before buyers could do their research over the Internet.

The problem with the current system is that it no longer applies in today's world. I used to joke that buyers are on the Internet looking at homes far more than their real estate agents are—but it's really not a joke anymore!

FACT: *Study shows a home is shown an average of 8 times before it sells—Thank you virtual tours!*

An old-time structure in a new-fangled age

I've been in this business for about three decades. I'd say that, thirty years ago, the agent's work deserved the commission. Back in the days before Al Gore invented the Internet, I wrote documents out by hand, picked up the MLS books every week, and hand-delivered contracts and listings.

These days, all my forms are online, and I don't have to do much more than fill in the blanks. I type things in, send them off, and talk to my clients (who have already done all the research online) by email and phone. Booking a trip on Expedia takes more time.

Think about it. Why should the commission structure stay the same when the business has changed so much? There is so much consumer-driven technology out there, influencing every other kind of business—yet the real estate industry is still sticking to a fossilized and inefficient way of selling your home.

What service does a real estate agent really provide for their fee today? I think the website ReallyRottenRealty [http://po.st/simplesold20] sums it up best: "We believe in the 3 Ps of real estate marketing: Put, Put and Pray. Put a sign in the yard, Put it on MLS, and then Pray someone will come along and buy it. We usually find that after enough time passes, and after several price drops, the house usually sells itself without too much intervention from us. That's an easy commission earned. We like easy." Signs, marketing, and marketing materials? *ListingDoor.com* has great marketing materials that are super easy to create.

Use the money you save for yourself and your family. Use it to pay down debt or treat yourself to something. Just don't waste it on a huge commission.

Your home is the single most valuable asset you own. For many people, their home represents the majority of their net worth.

Home sales by the numbers

There is another way to look at the agent's commission. What percentage of your equity does it represent? This is something homeowners often overlook, but it's very important. If you don't remember anything else from this book, remember this!

Here's an example of what I'm talking about. Let's say your home is worth $400,000 and your equity is $60,000. If you hire a real estate agent who charges 6 percent, and your home sells for $400,000, you end up paying the agent $24,000 in commission.

That's 40 percent of your equity! In commission! That's cutting your profit almost in half—and those are hard dollars that cannot be recouped. Yikes! That's $24,000 you could do a lot with.

What percentage of your equity would a real estate commission eat up? 30%, 40%, 50%, or more?

Take this same house, the one that's selling for $400,000 at $24,000 or 6 percent commission. In 2000, that house was probably worth $250,000. Isn't it a little unfair that your agent would make an extra

$9,000 just because your home value increased over time? Even taking the recession into account, real estate commission revenues have increased by huge amounts—in this case, 37 percent—even while the business has gotten dramatically easier because of the Internet. Real estate may be the last industry that hasn't been democratized by technology. Why should you care about this? Because it's hitting you where it hurts: in your equity.

Again, like your 401K, your home equity should only be touched in an emergency. It is likely part of your retirement savings. You've been tending to it for years; you paid the mortgage, the taxes, and the insurance. Why shouldn't you keep the full equity? In many real estate deals, the real estate agent is the only person to leave the closing with a check. Beware: as I said before, the broker makes you broker.

Let's take it a step further. Think about what you want from this transaction: you want your home to sell, and you want to come out of it alive financially. In a world completely driven by value, homes with inflated prices simply do not sell. If you're hoping that your real estate agent will magically find you a high–priced offer to compensate for the commission you're paying, you're wrong. If you set a high asking price, your house will probably stay on the market until you lower the price.

But no way is your real estate agent going to drop his or her commission! And with that 6 percent built into the pricing structure, you could easily lose any possibility of coming out of this deal in a good financial state.

The answer is simple. Sell your home yourself. Don't listen when anyone tells you that only a real estate agent can sell a home. It's what the National Association of REALTORS would have you believe. They exist to work against consumer interests. It's as if a Real Housewife met a snake oil salesman and had a brood of real estate agents for children. That's why you should take charge. If you have any doubts, turn on Bravo's Million Dollar Listing and tell me with a straight face that you can't do as good a job as they do.

Do agents earn all that money they make?

The bottom line about the real estate commission structure is that it works *against* the seller on every level. It's in an agent's best interest to accept the first decent offer that comes in for a house, regardless of whether it meets your needs. This is the industry secret that the book Freakonomics: A Rogue Economist Explores the Hidden Side of Everything [http://po.st/simplesold21] (written by University of Chicago professor of economics Steven D. Levitt and *New York Times* journalist Stephen J. Dubner) first revealed in 2005. It took up long-term residency on the Times best-seller list, and went on to sell more than 5 million copies in 35 languages. But real estate firms are still fighting to keep the public from seeing this truth.

Here's Freakonomics' example which was also featured in their 2010 documentary "Freakonomics: The Movie" (watch video clip). [http://po.st/simplesold22]

> For you, it would be economically worthwhile to hold your house an extra two weeks to make an extra $10,000. Assuming your real estate agent is charging a 6 percent commission, you'd receive $9,400 of that money, which is not bad for an extra two weeks' work. However, of the $600 left over for the commission, your agent's only going to receive about $150 after the buyer's agent and the real estate firm take their share. To the agent, $150 is scant pay for an extra two weeks of negotiations. It's pretty doubtful that your real estate

agent is going to go the extra mile in selling your home to get you that extra $10,000 when there are other houses to be sold and other commissions to earn.

Do you see why it pays for real estate agents to undermine their clients' best interests?

I love this business. I love working to make this huge, personal transaction go as smoothly as possible for my clients. The low–commission system I have used for years in my business has worked. I have never had to advertise to find clients. My listings are known for being priced according to the market—and they sell. But this book isn't about *my* business—it's about *yours.*

People need and deserve a choice. I've been waiting for years for the real estate industry to change. I was sure that when more houses started to sell on the Internet, the NAR would respond, and the current real estate agency system would shift to help the homeowner. You'd think the recession would have done it, if nothing else. But it hasn't happened.

Why has the NAR refused to support an MLS that's open to all homeowners? Many sellers are hurting and simply cannot afford to pay an exorbitant commission to get their home sold. Shame on the real estate industry for not coming together and coming up with a plan! People could have sold their homes and saved their credit.

But instead of offering their clients some relief, the industry stayed rigidly set in its ways and homeowners lost out. The NAR is the lone voice of the industry and we can't change them.

But we can remind ourselves that we have a choice.

You can do this. As an agent, I can assure you that I've dealt with more than one real estate agent who knew *less* about real estate than you do at this moment! They had absolutely *no idea* what they were doing. Thankfully, not all agents are like this. There are some great ones out there. But I can honestly say that only 8 percent of real estate agents are worth the commission. The other 92 percent—well, you know my thoughts on the matter.

The standards to be a real estate agent are so low; it's the biggest complaint among other agents. A recent study said that sellers would take 10% less not to hassle with an agent. I can assure you after reading this book you will be in the 8%—not the 92%.

When your agent is a liability

Sometimes an agent can actually interfere with a home sale. Agents are human beings with emotions, and those emotions can play into how they handle your sale. In order to get the best possible deal for your house, the transaction has to be 100 percent about how the buyer and seller feel. But the agent has feelings, too.

I knew an agent who hated another agent so much that she refused to show his listings. This is unethical, but it happens more often than you probably think. I have heard agents try to trash the reputation of other agents. I have seen them try to steal clients.

Last year, I was helping a man sell his home. The buyer seemed willing to pay the asking price—but the other agent wasn't! It took a few days to figure out what was happening. It had to do with a friendship between the other agent and the seller's ex–wife. There were emotions at play of which the buyer and seller were unaware. The deal was stalled because of the private agenda of the other agent!

Without the agent in the middle, the only emotions you'll have to consider will be the buyer's and your own. That's so much simpler.

The listing agent will return your call — eventually

Once you understand what an agent does—and doesn't do—you will see that there are great advantages to selling your home yourself.

One of the biggest marketing myths is that you have to be on call 24/7 during the process of selling your home. But wait! This is the Internet age, an age of convenience and savviness. Yes, you'll want to be easily reachable for your buyers—but isn't that better than being on the phone with your real estate agent all the time?

Buyers have adapted to the online marketplace and are now shopping for homes as if they were shopping for consumer electronics. They prefer to find out the information about a home on the Internet—and on their own schedule—instead of slowing things down by getting that information from a real estate agent or firm.

Buyers gather information and then decide which homes they want to see. Almost all of the clients I've seen lately will email the agent and say exactly which homes they want to see. The only thing the agency does is line up the showing and unlock the door.

The MLS is a service in which brokers pool their listings and establish procedures for sharing commissions. It's designed for agents, not for consumers. Zillow, Trulia, and Yahoo! Real Estate have superior technology and have the consumer in mind.

Buyers spend more time on these sites on average than on the MLS site because of the user-driven widgets: you can get local mortgage rates, sort by demographics and school systems, and much more. The MLS has tried to keep up by adding a considerable amount of do-it-yourself convenience—but when you find a place you like, you still have to schedule with a real estate agency in order to see it. This adds middlemen, and middlemen add commissions and hassle.

Think about the middlemen you encounter when buying a car. First, you deal with the salesman; then he has to get the manager to authorize giving you such a good deal; then you have to talk to the finance guy (even if you are paying cash!) Five hours later, you can buy the car. It makes you want to scream, "JUST SELL ME THE CAR!" And don't you always leave just a little skeptical about whether or not you got a fair deal?

FACT: *Gallup's Honesty and Ethics Poll ranks real estate agents below bankers and just above politicians!*

Simple and SOLD was designed to give you the personal control that's been missing from real estate transactions. As an example, consider the way you schedule appointments online.

Let's say you have three appointment requests on a Saturday. If those three appointments were scheduled through a real estate firm, they'd just be scheduled with no regard to your convenience, working around not only the buyers' schedules but also the schedules of their agents. One appointment might be at 10:00, another at 2:00 and another at 4:45. You wouldn't be able to leave your house all day!

With *Simple and SOLD*, you communicate directly with the buyers. You can schedule those appointments thirty minutes apart if you like, leaving the rest of your day free to go about your business.

If you've ever tried to sell your home with a real estate agency before, you know the frustration that comes from having to keep your home show–ready at all hours and days of the week. You have zero control over their schedule, and they often give you no more than fifteen minutes notice. This is one of the most common complaints that real estate agencies receive, which is not surprising; most of us do not like to be caught in our pajamas when business is on the table. Go figure.

I have lost patience with real estate agencies on many occasions because of problems scheduling appointments. Say I have a client who's fallen in love with a particular house and is willing to pay the listing price or close to it. I'll call the listing agent to try to set up an appointment for my buyer, but the agent will fail to call me back. I'll call her office directly, only to find out that no one else can show the home except the listing agent, who's unfortunately out of town and out of contact.

FACT: *You are more invested in selling your home than anyone.*

My client will move on to a different home, the agent will return from her vacation, and the house will go "sale pending" a week later—for $50,000 less than the listing price. The homeowners will never know that they missed out on potential buyers while their agent was on vacation, and they'll never know that those buyers would have paid so much more.

It's also not unusual to call the real estate office's appointment number—not the main number, but the one real estate agents list on the MLS to set appointments—and get a recording saying, "All of our agents are helping other clients. The next available agent will be with you shortly." Shortly means two songs later from the on–hold music selection.

You'll eventually get a human on the phone, but they'll tell you that they're booked and have no one on "desk duty" to handle your call and set up your appointment. Can you imagine being a seller and knowing that your own potential buyers are being treated this way? It's more convenient for large firms to have designated appointment numbers, but buyers and sellers end up missing out.

Using lock boxes is becoming a huge trend. An agent puts a lockbox on the home and contracts with a third–party service to schedule the appointments. This is done under the pretense that the third–party scheduling service gets you more showings. I like these services because typically you get a human being on the phone, or you can schedule the appointment online. However, all the agent does is list the home and then wait for a buyer. That's not much service for a commission of 6 percent or more! You can use a lockbox too, and you can do it even if you're still living in the home. We'll explain how in a later chapter.

Here's a funny blog named "Did My Agent Go Into The Witness Protection Plan?" [http://po.st/simplesold23] that was written by a homeowner describing how she thought her agent went into the witness protection plan after she signed the listing agreement.

You are the best agent for the home you love

By being directly involved with your buyer, you'll also control the feedback. This area of the transaction is often overlooked, but I can't emphasize enough how important it is. Your transaction will be so much smoother if feedback on the house is controlled and directed by the person who understands the house best—you!

Let me give you an example. A buyer was looking at a lot I had listed for a house he wanted to build. He had narrowed his search down to three potential lots. Because I'm a one–woman business with personal knowledge of the community where his top pick was located—rather than the property desk at the real estate firm or the agent that had property duty that day (who had no interest in making the sale)—the transaction took on a completely different tone.

I was able to talk directly to the buyer. "In a perfect world," I asked him, "what would you be looking for?"

He said, "We want to see children playing on the street and riding bikes."

Because of his answer, I knew the neighborhood was perfect for him, and I knew that I had the tools to control the feedback and close the deal. I told him to drive by the cul-de-sac where his lot was located on a Saturday. I knew he would see the kids on their Big Wheels and bicycles there. He bought the property the next week!

You know your home and your neighborhood better than anyone, and definitely better than any real estate agent. The schools, the neighbors, the nearby parks, the path where you go on walks with your kids—you know what's special about your property. At the very least, you surely remember why you bought this home that you're now trying to sell!

What are your own experiences worth? The stories and images you present about your home are there to justify your price. In any market, a well-priced home is the key to getting it sold. It may be flawlessly maintained, it may be a fixer-upper—no matter the specifics, there's a price out there that will make your home the star of the market. Your role is simply to identify its best qualities and find the perfect price. Once you start harnessing the Internet's possibilities, common sense and a little business knowledge will take you the rest of the way. Use the Internet to tell the story and establish a direct buyer-seller relationship. You're more likely to control the story and the outcome once the buyer sees you're directly involved.

When you're in charge of the sale, your relationship with the buyer will become a partnership. Your common goal—the successful sale of the house you both love—will become the most important thing to both of you. By controlling and directing the feedback from the beginning, the ball will be in your court. That will allow you to do more to make the process go smoothly.

Change and moving are always stressful. I wouldn't want to lie to you and say that selling your home this way will magically rid you of the stress of transition. But you will experience much less heartache over all of it if you retain control of the situation. You'll always be up–to–date. You won't have to depend on a weekly written report; you'll know exactly how much effort is being put into the marketing, so you won't have the frustration of wondering, "What is being done for me?"

Bottom Lines:

1. The housing market has changed completely.
2. Selling your house yourself makes more sense now than in the past.
3. The Internet has tools to help you.
4. The serious advantages to selling your house yourself include convenience and the ability to offer feedback.
5. You're the best agent for your home, because you know and love it more than anyone.
6. The average home is shown 8 times before it is sold.

"Companion Workbook" Download
http://po.st/workbook22

Chapter 3

WHAT'S MY HOUSE WORTH, ANYWAY?

If you think someone might fall in love with your house and offer you more than it's worth—think again. Buyers are extremely educated. I repeat, buyers are *extremely educated.*

I do not care where you are located or what year you bought your house, or even how much money you spent to fix it up. Your house is not worth what you think it should sell for—it's worth what comparable houses have sold for in the past sixty to ninety days, what are called *comps* in the industry

This applies even if your house is the only one for sale for miles around. It applies even if you bought it in 2007, a year many real estate transactions were made.

So, what is your house worth? It's worth what it's worth. That's your starting point.

You don't have to suffer from "analysis paralysis" to get the information you need. I'll show you how. Just remember that in my experience, houses that are priced at what they're worth (according to the above definition) sell for within 4 percent of their asking price.

Houses that aren't priced at what they're worth get within 9 percent of their price—but only after it has been reduced to the market price. Those properties are on the market much longer. If you overprice your house, it will cost you!

Let's say your home is worth $500,000 but you want to price it at $550,000 because you think buyers want to negotiate. I have seen this scenario numerous times. What ends up happening is your home will eventually get reduced to $500,000 but it has been on the market so long, buyers think they can negotiate a lower price. After you reduce it, you end up getting offers that are low but if you would have priced it on the market, you would have had offers close to your asking price. Again, homes priced on the market typically sell for within 4% of the asking price, and overpriced homes get reduced and sell within 9% of the asking price. With a $500,000 home, that can be over $22,000.

You, the appraiser

Technically, an appraisal is a formal estimate of the value of your home as determined by a state–certified appraiser. Note the words "formal" and "state–certified." Appraisals are a matter of fact–based judgment, not of subjective opinion.

Talking to a friend who dabbles in real estate is not going to work here, and neither is consulting with your neighbors. But that doesn't mean that you can't do the job yourself with some preparation and education.

Start doing homework online about two months before you plan to put your home on the market. A good place to begin is by going to Trulia or Zillow. When they show a new listing that sold immediately, there's a very high probability that the home sold for list price or close to list price. You can also search comparable home sales in your area. My site, *ListingDoor.com*, offers an IntelReport that gives you all the information you need to price your home. It has an Automated Price Value but I also suggest using the 3 pricing keys found in this chapter to tweak your price.

Many real estate firms will email you information about area sales for free, in hopes of persuading you to list with them. If you do this, keep in mind that you'll probably be getting emails and phone calls from them for weeks after the initial contact.

You might get a real estate agent calling you to say that they have a buyer for you. They'll ask if you're willing to pay the commission for the buyer's agent, meaning that you'd pay half of the normal real estate commission. Be sure to clarify the exact amount of commission they're talking about so you can make an educated decision.

Crunch the numbers. If they pencil out, consider paying the half commission. You'll still be saving a lot of money, your holding costs will be less, and you'll get to skip some steps in the sales process. Time and money will often make it worthwhile—but do the calculations to be sure. The numbers don't lie.

When you're analyzing other homes online, use features like video tours to get a good idea of what buyers out there are looking at right now. Pay close attention to other homes' selling prices versus their listing prices, and note how long it took them to sell. (The phrase "priced to sell" is a cliché that should generally be avoided, but it contains a nugget of truth: you'll find that homes sell faster and closer to their listing price if they're priced for the market from the beginning.)

Maybe you live in one of the few states that are still in the "non-disclosure" category, which means that the MLS calls sales information "proprietary" to keep it from becoming public record. There aren't many of these states left, and I think that market pressure and legal cases will get them to change in the near future. But with all the methods listed above, you can still find the information you need, regardless of which state you live in.

Although you can do most of your analysis using the information you find online, you should also do some work on the ground. Visit a few open houses and take notes. With every home you look at—whether online or in real life—compare their square footage, condition, curb appeal, renovations, and neighborhood to your own home and neighborhood. Collect the same information on each property; use the form on the *ListingDoor.com* website to organize it all and make sure you haven't left anything out.

This is what real estate firms call a "comparative market analysis" or CMA, but you'll be taking *all* the important factors into account. A lot of the information out there neglects the importance of consumption (how many homes per month are selling in your price range) when calculating your price. Experience taught me never to forget this factor.

But the house down the street *never* sold!

The US housing market has recovered from the recession, but if your neighborhood was hit particularly hard during the slump, you might have seen a "fire sale" effect where prices on foreclosed homes put a downward pressure on prices across the board. Those foreclosures are what I call "anchor sales." They sold or will sell at very low prices, but they keep all the prices in the neighborhood down at levels that may just not work for you. Don't let the presence of foreclosures bring you down with the prices. We all know that the recession hit in places we never expected. But be smart about this. Most markets have recovered. You don't want your home's value to be dragged down by the extremely low prices of foreclosures around you, so it might pay to wait until the foreclosures sell and *then* put your home on the market.

FACT: *Not all foreclosures are going for giveaway prices.*

However, there are exceptions. Remember that not all foreclosed homes are going for a giveaway price. The ones that are incredibly cheap are usually stripped of almost everything and are being sold as chassis—because some evicted families take the cabinets, the plumbing fixtures, and other things with them when they leave. If there are any foreclosures selling at prices close to your own asking price, you're ready to go!

Remember, too, that for a buyer to get a loan, your home has to be appraised taking three or four months of past sales in the neighborhood into account. You'll get a much better price if you can get these foreclosed houses out of the equation.

If you really need to get your home out on the market regardless of foreclosures, then head this issue off immediately in your marketing materials. Let your buyers know in one quick paragraph that houses selling for below market price in the area were likely foreclosures that were probably stripped, and as such the banks had to sell them as quickly as possible.

Buyers will appreciate that you told them about it rather than simply hoping they wouldn't find out. Trying to keep information from a buyer is a common move in real estate transactions, but it's one that ultimately backfires.

Should I get a formal appraisal?

If you're busy and don't have time to do the research to find your market value, then by all means, hire an appraiser. But take a look at *ListingDoor.com*'s IntelReport before you do. The information there is the same information that appraisers use so you might be able to save yourself the trouble and expense. However, even if you've done your own analysis, you can hire an appraiser to confirm the data you've gathered.

Appraisers are third–party experts trained to determine the value of homes. Having an official, professional opinion on your home's price can help you although it's not a must. Throughout this process, people will offer their opinions on what your home is worth, but almost all of this advice will be subjective and misleading. The appraiser's opinion will be a professional one.

There are two reliable associations for appraisers: Appraisal Institute [http://po.st/simplesold24] and American Society of Appraisers [http://po.st/simplesold25]. When you're choosing an appraiser, be sure to ask questions. For which mortgage companies or banks do the appraisers work? How many homes in the area have they appraised in the last year? What factors do they consider in their appraisal? Will they verify the square footage of your home? Do they know your neighborhood? Will they be available to answer questions after they do the appraisal? You want to ensure that your appraiser is thorough and thoughtful.

Be cautious if your potential appraiser is already trying to get off the phone after you ask these questions. You want an appraiser who will take their time assessing the value of your home. Good service means good business.

Know that most appraisers can do what is called the "mini–appraisal." These aren't full–blown appraisals, and they're typically used when you're getting a home equity loan or refinancing. Mini–appraisals should give you a fair price to ask for your home; they're usually cheaper and have a quicker turnaround than a full–scale appraisal.

If you already have an appraisal, but it's a few years old, ask how much it will cost to update it — it'll usually cost less than a new appraisal. But you should never use an appraisal that's more than six months old to set your listing price. Home values can swing significantly in less than a year. If you do not know the square footage of your home, you can hire an appraiser for a few hundred dollars to measure your home. You do not have to get a full appraisal from the appraiser. It is important to have the correct square footage — it is a factor in determining price.

When the appraiser comes, he or she will do a market analysis and a site inspection that considers the physical features of your home: age, lot size, square footage, construction quality, and so on. A few days later, you'll get your estimate. It's not that different from what you'd do applying the same techniques—the 3 golden keys to pricing that you find later in this chapter. But the fact that the appraisal is from a professional can help you when dealing with buyers. It will keep you confident in your price when dealing with hagglers.

If you price it right, they will come

Getting an idea of what your house is worth is the first step in arriving at a reasonable asking price. Perhaps the most important aspect of control you'll gain here is that you'll be able to set a fair and accurate price yourself—a price that you will negotiate yourself and back up personally with market-based evidence.

Anyone can search homes in any area and sort them by price, analyzing the data as they go; using the Internet to determine the value of your home is a matter of forensics. Do your readers know what this means in this context?

Pricing is both an art and science. In many ways, it relies on simple business sense, but in other ways, it relies on knowledge of the buyer, the community, and the timing of the transaction. While all these things should be a part of the home selling process, many real estate agents don't go to all this trouble. It's not their home; they're just trying to get their commission and get out.

You need to know the value of your house before you can determine an asking price. You don't want to make the mistake of putting a huge price on your house. A too–high price sends a clear message: "We don't know what's really going on in the market right now."

Home buyers today will have an idea of the value of your house, and they will want to get down to business. Sure, the Internet's given them a lot of tools and the market is set for good deals, but the buyers are still feeling the effects of the recession personally, just like everybody else. They're guarding their money. They're looking for a good investment, and they know they have to find a home that works for their circumstances and finances long term.

They have been working hard to educate themselves about their various options. At the very least, they have spent some time sorting through the current of homes on the market. I guarantee you that buyers today will not deal with sellers whose thinking isn't grounded in market realities.

FACT: *Realistic pricing brings serious buyers.*

Let's get another myth out of the way. A real estate agent isn't going to somehow find a loophole in the market and sell your home for way more than it's currently worth. Some like to name big, inflated prices. Real estate agents may assure their potential clients that their homes are worth boom prices, but this is partly flattery and salesmanship, and partly a way to snag the seller as a client.

Some real estate firms teach their agents to take their listings at a high price and walk the client down once they're locked in. Unfortunately, this technique doesn't consider the actual value of the property—so don't let an agent's high number give you an unrealistic idea about value. Even if they list your house at an incredibly high price, they'll accept a low offer for you and tell you it's the smartest move you could make. It's fun to dream sometimes, but pricing your home is not the time for dreaming.

Price your house too high, and you're giving your neighbors a powerful tool to help them sell *their* house at a fair price. You're also putting blood in the water for the sharks waiting for you to lower your price.

Even if your home is a beautiful and desirable property, buyers won't come to look at it if they think the price is unreasonably high. They'll wait for the reduction you'll inevitably make so that you can get it sold. In the meantime, you'll end up with what real estate agents refer to as a "stale home."

Your home is anything but stale; so don't price it to seem so.

This is a great blog on "How the Real Estate Market Has Gone From Inefficient To Efficient". [http://po.st/simplesold26]

The 3 Golden Keys of Pricing

If you remember anything from this chapter, remember this section.

There are three things I keep in mind in every single one of my transactions when I'm evaluating a home and setting its asking price with the seller. They are the secret of my success and the reason countless other real estate agents and customers have called me over the years to ask, "How did you get that listing to sell?"

The three concepts, or as I call them the "3 golden keys" are simple and vital for anyone who wants to understand how real estate pricing works. They are based of *ListingDoor.com*'s IntelReport; my easy–to–understand roadmap to a fair market–based listing price for your home. It makes the process super, super easy.

#1: Competition. A home seller might try to inflate their home's price, thinking that they need to set the bar high before they negotiate. Or they might have a real estate agent who wants the listing so badly that she'll tell them whatever they want to hear. But in doing this, that home seller is putting himself at a severe competitive disadvantage.

It's like a football game: you must know the competition. How many homes in your price range are on the market? If there are several homes in your neighborhood waiting to sell, you must price your home aggressively—read: a little less than you might have liked—in order to get the buyers.

Keep in mind, the amount you come down in price is probably equal to or less than a month's worth of carrying costs, which is the amount you'll pay if you hold the home for longer.

If there are fewer homes in your neighborhood for sale, then you can shoot for a price that's right on the market.

#2: Consumption. Now that you know how many homes in your price range are available, find out how many homes have been selling each month for the last three to six months. This will give you what is called the "absorption rate" or rate of attrition. This number gives you a clear picture of how long it will likely take you to sell your home. It's not a guessing game; it's a business calculation.

#3: Condition. How does your home's condition compare to other homes on the market and the ones that have sold? Be realistic. What is the condition of the landscaping? How about the exterior paint or updates? What's the condition of the carpet, flooring, appliances, roof, and interior paint?

Evaluate your home the way a picky buyer would and have realistic expectations.

Making the important final adjustments

Now that you have a sense of your home's value, you need to

start thinking as a seller to get your final price.

But before you go any further, remember that you should not try to set a listing price based on what other sellers are *asking for* their property. You need to think in terms of *selling price only.* HGTV even had a show (five season–60 episodes) about this called Real Estate Intervention [http://po.st/simplesold27] which is all about sellers who overprice!

The price at which you list and ultimately sell your home has to be in line with actual sales. In my roughly three decades of experience in real estate, I have fought this battle with sellers constantly.

"Well, my friend Judy is asking "X" amount for her home, and my home is worth more than hers!" a client will say. Well, Judy is under the illusion that we're still in 2007. She will have her house on the market for two years at that price, and she'll end up lowering the asking price eventually.

It's an undeniable fact that houses priced on the market sell for more. Homes that are overpriced typically cost the seller an additional 5 to 9 percent, and the loss could be even more if holding costs are high.

FACT: *Overpricing will cost you.*

By researching final selling prices, you'll see how many homes sell per month in your area and in your price range. That will give you an idea of the actual value of your house on today's market.

A few years ago a doctor called me to list his house. I told him what it would sell for—$700,000. He was furious and told me he would never list with me, that the bait and real estate firm had given him a listing price of $950,000 so of course he went with that firm. Well, guess what? The home did not sell for more than a year, and then the stock market fell. Oh, no—the good doctor ended up selling 18 months later, for $610,000 because that was now the market price. Trust me, this is a very common — and costly — scenario.

Once you've established an asking price, look at the difference between the sold homes and your home and adjust the price. If you have access to the original asking prices of these homes, you'll notice significant discrepancies. That means the sellers were bargained down from their asking price.

As I said earlier, you'll also notice homes whose selling prices are very close to their asking prices. Those will be the homes that were priced thoughtfully, in line with the market and close to their actual value. These homes sell faster and with much less fuss than homes whose seller started out highballing.

Bottom Lines:

1. Determining the value of your house is the first step in setting the price.
2. Research what comparable homes have sold for—*not* what they listed for.
3. Competition, attrition, and condition will figure into the value.
4. You can calculate approximately what your house is worth—or you can hire a professional appraiser to get you started.

"Companion Workbook" Download
http://po.st/workbook22

Chapter 4

HOW WILL I KNOW WHAT SOMEONE IS WILLING TO PAY?

The best analogy I can think of for pricing a home is this: we all have an idea of what $20 is worth. If you had a $20 bill and asked a friend to buy it from you for $24, he would say no. In fact, if you offered the $20 bill for $21, he would still say no. But if you asked him to buy a $20 bill for $19.99, he would almost certainly say yes.

That is how pricing a home works. Every buyer will have an idea of what they think your house is worth. They'll never, ever pay more than that. But if they think they can buy your house for just slightly less than it's worth, they will buy it.

During my decades in real estate, I have experienced two recessions and two housing bubbles. I've also seen some firsts, many of them this year. I'm writing this book to share information that is truly up–to–the–minute, based on my experience selling houses last year. It's a different real estate market than it was even a few years ago.

Be the bride, not the bridesmaid

Pricing a house is both a forensic science and a fine art. In some ways, it's a matter of sharp objectivity. You start by using an appraisal (whether done by you or a professional) to get an accurate, precise picture of your home's value. Then you have to crunch some more data to see whether your holding costs and days on the market mean that you should further adjust your home's price.

You want to sell quickly, and you want your selling price to be as close to your asking price as possible. Why? Well, take it from me, a Texas woman: Everyone wants to be the bride and no one wants to be the bridesmaid.

Selling a home is much the same way. Your home, in order to stand out and be successful in a tough market, has to be the bride. It has to be special, set apart, and the object of every buyer's admiration and affection! And these days, the best way to win them over is to present them with an eye-catching asking price.

If you haven't already done this, you should adjust your price so that it will grab buyers' attention and keep it. Yes, this often means going just a little lower— even $500—but time and time again, this strategy pays off in the long run.

How long does it take to sell a house?

You can predict how long it will take your house to sell by evaluating your Days On Market (DOM) and adjusting your price accordingly.

Here's an example. Say that, in your competitive market, there is one home selling every thirty days. That means that in order to be the home that is selected for purchase, you've got to be priced *ahead of* everyone to sell in the first thirty days. You've got to be in second place to sell in sixty days, and in third place to sell in ninety days. It's that simple.

If there are ten homes in your price range, we know that you have ten months' worth of inventory. If you need to sell quickly for financial reasons, then you need to go ½ to 1 percent below the appraisal price, so your house will be perceived as a good value. This also creates a sense of urgency with potential buyers. Better you drop your price and sell your home than let your neighbor beat you to it! Get ahead of the game. With ten homes on the market, someone is going to drop their price.

Not calculating your DOM can lead you into an unnecessarily awful situation. Here's a story to illustrate this cold reality:

A bank once asked me to go take a look at a home that a builder was having a hard time selling. The home was priced at $1.5 million because that was the loan balance!

As always, I used the 3 golden keys:

Competition: To find this, I looked at how many homes were currently for sale at that price. I saw that sixteen builders had similar spec homes on the market.

Consumption: I researched how many homes had sold at that price in the past year, and found two.

Condition: The house's condition was perfect, with new construction.

The DOM here was *huge*; if no one dropped his price, these houses would take a full eight years or more to sell! Why in the world did the banker lending the money not look at this?

My real estate knowledge wasn't even necessary in this case; all I needed to figure this situation out was common sense. The builder's asking price might have corresponded to the market average, but the terrible DOM factor meant that he would have to lower that price if he wanted to sell within the next two presidential administrations.

What does it cost to not sell a house?

Even if you're not in a hurry to sell, you need to be aware of your monthly holding costs. They can eat at your equity and really hurt you financially.

Calculate mortgage payments, taxes, and insurance per month, and realize that each month you hold on to this home is one more month you are on the hook for these costs. It often makes more sense to quickly lower the price in order for your home to become the "bride" of the market.

Think about it. If you end up sitting on a high price for ninety or 120 days or more, even if you end up getting "top dollar," your profit has been eaten up by holding costs you've already spent.

Additionally, the longer a home sits on the market, the more it tells the buyer that there's plenty of room to negotiate. And by that point, there probably is!

The most important factor in pricing: You

Understanding local economic and social factors will help you predict what type of buyer will end up calling your place home when the ink dries. Has a big company recently moved into or out of the neighborhood? Is your area growing or are people moving away? Are the homes for sale mostly newer or older than yours? You can use all of these factors to tailor your marketing and price so that you more directly target the buyers you want.

Remember that the context surrounding your asking price has to do with you as well—not just the market. Are you being transferred for work, or do you need to sell for other reasons? Are you looking to buy a new home as you sell your old one? Maybe the neighborhood that you're moving to has lower real estate prices than your current neighborhood. All of these things can affect your asking price.

If you're dealing with financial stressors and need to sell quickly, you might want to set your price up to 1 percent lower than the prices of comparable homes on the market in your neighborhood. Remember, you're already saving money by not paying a commission. Figure out how much of these savings you can apply to the price of your home to achieve a faster sale.

There's only one scenario in which a slightly higher asking price might serve you: there's not a lot of inventory on the market in your area, and you're okay waiting to sell. In that case, price it 2 to 4 percent above market price. In all other cases—lots of other homes on the market, anchor sales holding prices down, financial constraints pressuring you to sell quickly—get ahead of the curve by pricing your home to sell quickly and well.

Go tell it on the mountain—but not quite yet

So now you have arrived at your perfect listing price. The timing is right and you're ready to put your home out there for the world to see.

Not so fast! You'll want to prepare all your marketing materials before you actually get your home on the market. We'll talk about that in the next chapter. But here's one last thing about pricing that you might want to take into account as you give your price a final evaluation.

Listing websites have price filters in increments of $10,000, $50,000, and $100,000, depending on the price range. If you're close to one of these thresholds, it might be a good idea to drop down so that you reach a wider audience.

For example, if you're listing your home for $410,000, dropping down to $400,000 will give you approximately 7 percent more viewers. Dropping the price to take advantage of a wider audience can be a good idea, especially if you need to move fast. You'll sell your home faster, and you'll save that $10,000 or more on mortgage payments, taxes, and insurance.

This may sound a bit unconventional—actually, it probably sounds really unconventional! But it's what you have to do to compete in today's market. Price your home so you get a fair price for it, but price it so it will sell.

Remember: Buyers are educated. You don't want to saddle yourself with "seller's anxiety" after four to six months of having no one bite on your high listing price—and then end up lowering the price to something even lower than you would have chosen initially.

Bottom Lines:

1. Many factors will influence your final asking price, and research will help you find these factors.
2. Pricing is both an art and a science, but it's not rocket science.
3. Use the 3 golden keys (Competition, Consumption, and Condition) to price your home.
4. Your reward for research will be a price that sells your home.

"Companion Workbook" Download
http://po.st/workbook22

Chapter 5

HOW CAN I MAKE MY HOUSE SEEM LIKE IT'S WORTH THIS PRICE?

Amy had great taste. Every night, she would lie in bed with her laptop and look for a cool house to buy. Amy and her husband were expecting their second child and needed a home with more space.

Amy looked at hundreds of houses, but kept going back to one that had been on the market for 240 days. The pictures of the house were awful—everything looked dark and smudgy and drab. But you can't judge a book by its cover—right?

"Look at this one, honey," she said to her husband. "It has a lot of the things we're looking for, even though the pictures are pretty bad …."

"I don't know," her husband said. "To me, that house just screams 'foreclosure'! They couldn't even afford a good camera—it looks like they shot those pictures with somebody's cell phone!"

Amy decided to follow her instincts and go see the house. Turns out, it was a great house that actually needed only cosmetic repairs.

The asking price was $950,000—but there had been no offers. Amy offered $750,000 and they got the house for $775,000. The only reason they were able to get such a great deal was because the photos of that house were so bad nobody else asked to see it!

Here's the punch line: Three years later, Amy and her husband decided they wanted to be closer to their kids' school, so they put the house on the market—with great photographs. It sold for $1.3 million.

FACT: *Quality photos make a huge difference.*

How would a big real estate firm market your home? The answer is: it depends!

Have you seen MLS listings where the house looked blurry and out of focus? Have you seen photos that show dirty dishes on the kitchen counter or bathroom photos that look like a toilet bowl ad? A real estate agent should make sure your home is represented in its best light, but that's not always what happens. That's why you have to be the marketing expert in this project.

Your agent will give you a standard description in a big pile of listings and a yard sign printed with the firm's name in big letters. In my mind, they ought to be paying you for advertising their business!

That marketing approach is generic and devoid of any real information that will get a buyer interested in your home quickly. And hasn't it been done that way since your grandparents bought a home? A big-name agency might seem to have initial benefits, but in the end, your real estate agent is still a stranger communicating with your buyers. Agents can't know your home and neighborhood the way that you do.

Savvy marketing will really set you apart from the rest of the crowd. Look at it as an amazing opportunity to give this transaction some WOW factor!

Get ready—get *really* ready

First and most importantly, do it right and don't hurry. The first two to three weeks that your home is on the market are crucial. Do not put your home on the market until everything's completely dialed in and ready.

By the time your very first prospective buyer contacts you, you should have all your facts in place and your comprehensive marketing materials prepared. Your home should be clean and ready to show with a shiny yard sign out front. (By the way, a good sign is very important. We'll talk about that in the next chapter. You can view examples of great yard signs on the *ListingDoor.com* website. You can also get a custom sign, but don't put it up just yet.)

If your house doesn't seem ready, buyers will be turned off by your lack of preparation and your home will sit on the market while you scramble to set up a good open house. And as I've said in the previous chapters about price, too much time on the market leads to a perception that something's "wrong" with your home, which makes your home much harder to sell. Prepare beforehand and avoid this altogether.

Start creating your marketing materials by gathering the facts. You can refer to a checklist on *ListingDoor.com*'s website. Start putting together a folder (physical or on your computer) with all the information you'll need.

Measure the important rooms in your home, and do it conservatively: if you have a built–in bookshelf, for example, measure from that bookshelf to the opposite wall instead of from wall to wall. You want to measure the living room, the kitchen, the dining room, the bedrooms, and any extra rooms you might have such as a playroom or study.

Remember, the square footage is the first marker of a home's value. And your buyer's going to want to know if their rug is going to fit!

Putting your best photo forward

Great photos are absolutely crucial to selling your home. Any digital camera should be fine; just make sure you upload your shots in high resolution. To make them look more professional, use the basic editing tools available on your computer's image software. Some of their automatic functions will adjust your light levels to make any photo look great.

Not confident in your ability to take good photos? For a modest charge, you can hire a professional firm to photograph your home; you can find them on the Internet.

When preparing your home for the photos, just tidy up like you're trying to impress someone. This will be the first of several cleaning frenzies, but they get easier each time.

Here's a list of tips to follow before the photos are taken:

1) Clean up **all** clutter. This is the most important thing you can do.
2) Have good light. Open the drapes, turn on lamps, and make sure all bulbs are working.
3) Turn off ceiling fans, because they can make weird blurs in some photos.
4) Put away all personal items in the bathroom.
5) Take everything off your counters, take the magnets off your fridge, and hide the pet bowls when you photograph your kitchen. Hide the pets, too.
6) If you have workout equipment in the living room, remove it!
7) If you have young children, their stuff is probably everywhere. High chairs, baby gates – all of this has to be removed, for the photo session.

8) Before photographing the exterior, trim the trees, mow the lawn, and blow away the fallen leaves. Put away the garden hoses, trash/recycling cans, and hide the sign for your security company. Move cars if parked in front of the house.
9) Clean the pool if you have one. Make sure there are no toys lying around.
10) If you have anything overtly political or seasonal in plain view, put it away before anyone shoots the photos. I have a great blog on this called "Animal Heads Sabotage Home Sales" [http://po.st/simplesold28]

3 Br, 2 Ba, charming — Zzzzzzz ...

Just as I was settling into the recliner with a bowl of popcorn, my old college roommate, Nancy in Missouri, called me for advice.

"We're trying to sell our house, and I wanted to know what you thought of this ad: 'Home for sale. Charming 3 bedroom, 2 baths, great neighborhood, close to shopping and amenities'. Does that sound all right?"

"Sounds to me like you're hiding something," I replied.

"What do you mean? This house *is* charming," Nancy said, beginning to choke up. "We *love* this house ...."

"I love your house too! But your ad doesn't have any pizzazz, and you're using those cliché adjectives," I explained gently. "Charming. Spacious. Those are general terms that people use when they don't have anything *real* to brag about."

I gave Nancy a moment to stop sniffling and asked, "What's your very favorite part of your house?"

"Well, I love the granite countertops, and we just put in a restaurant-style stove," she replied. "Hal wired the family room with a new sound system and installed maple flooring. You know, if he wasn't getting transferred, we'd stay here...."

"So, I suggested, "How about '3 bedrooms, 2 baths, granite and gourmet kitchen, maple flooring, state–of–the–art entertainment room'. See the difference?"

Nancy hung up to rework her ad. She seemed grateful. I wondered if she'd ever gotten over that nail–biting problem she had back in school ...."

Fantastic, spacious, and nondescript

Freakonomics revealed a dirty little secret about real estate marketing code words: real estate agents sometimes use generic words as subconscious shorthand to indicate that a house is worth less than its asking price. "Fantastic," "spacious," "charming," and "great neighborhood" all appear to be glowing descriptions of the homes they describe. However, authors Steven Levitt and Stephen Dubner found that these adjectives actually correlated with significantly lowered sales prices. They're non–specific and nondescript, and whether you (or the real estate agent) know it or not, they signify to buyers that the house lacks unique qualities—or worse, that there's something to hide.

The words that *Freakonomics* found to correlate with high sales prices were specific and visual: "granite," "maple," "gourmet," "state–of–the–art." Use this as a lesson. Be specific and don't hide anything. There's nothing worse than a buyer who feels misled.

> **FACT:** *In real estate as well as in life, it's important to choose your words carefully.*

You want to use simple yet very descriptive words, words that will really give a sense of the character of your home. Avoid clichés. In fact, avoid them "like the plague," which is another cliché.

The thing that will set you apart from the big real estate firms is that you talk like a real person and not an advertisement. You can find a middle ground between a totally boring description and one that includes overblown words like "sun–splashed." You do this by focusing on telling a story.

Storytelling is one of the most overlooked aspects of marketing. When real estate agents neglect to take this into account, the process becomes impersonal and prolonged, and that's no fun for anyone. It's a fact: you must tell the story of the home in order to make it special. Make your ad interesting. Reach that perfect middle ground by focusing on telling a story.

Don Draper on the TV show *Mad Men* once said, "Advertising is based on one thing: happiness." Tell your potential buyers how happy you were in your home over the years. Why did you buy it? Was it a good fit for you and your family? Why?

Tell the buyer about the uniquely wonderful times you've had there and they'll immediately begin to imagine *their* future happiness in your home—which is exactly what you want to make a sale.

I suggest that at the very onset of your marketing phase, you sit down and write a short story about why you love your home. If you lack that creative gene, find a friend who has it. Bribe them with dinner and a glass of wine and shove some paper in front of them. You can incorporate this story into your marketing materials.

A few words can make all the difference. I just sold a home to buyers from out of town. I explained to them that everyone knew each other on the street, and the neighbors were all friends. As I put it, "This is a home where people drop in." That was important to them because they were moving from out of town, from a house on an isolated street.

Those few words showed them that making friends in their new town would be easy. It ended up being a perfect new beginning for them.

What if my house doesn't have a story?

If you get stuck trying to tell your house's story, think about what you'd say if you were bragging about the house to an old friend. Talking it over with someone can help you clarify your feelings about the house and put them into words. Your house does have a story, even if it doesn't spring immediately to mind.

I had a client in Houston whose home was on a semi–busy corner in a residential neighborhood. She built the home, and I was surprised she had chosen a lot on a corner. "Why did you buy that house?" I asked.

She said she loved that corner because the neighbors walked up and down the sidewalk, and she would wave to them from her kitchen sink. It was like living in a small town instead of the city.

What a great story! It showed why her home was such a special find. The location was now a huge positive that set the home apart from all others in the area.

Sometimes a home's story is as simple as the kind of neighbors you have. Sometimes it's a little bit of history. And sometimes it has to do with the loving work you've put into the building, or the wonderful times you've had there.

Know your house's history and be ready to share it like a friendly storyteller—beginning with the right ad.

Bottom Lines:

1. You're the most qualified person to market your home.
2. You'll need good photographs, so clean up your house and get some.
3. Write your house's story and use that story to create a good ad.
4. Start a folder to hold all your marketing materials, either real or online.

"Companion Workbook" Download
http://po.st/workbook22

Chapter 6

DOES THIS MEAN PEOPLE WILL BE COMING OVER?

If you apply everything I've talked about in this chapter, your marketing and customer service for your house will be top-notch. In my opinion, just being personable and gracious will set your home apart from other houses being sold by disinterested real estate agents. Buyers will know that you are not settling for the conventional way of selling your home.

Remember this: the agent's percentage of commission stays the same, no matter what the value of the home is. Do you think the guy with a million-dollar home gets $60,000 worth of marketing and customer service? Do you think the guy with a $200,000 home gets his $12,000 worth? What a real estate firm does is exactly what is in this book and more.

Now that you've accumulated some photos and other marketing tools—and you're committed to marketing this home yourself—you'll save the commission. It's time to earn that savings. The price you pay will be a little of your time and energy.

Where should I list my home?

I've already mentioned the biggest real estate websites: Zillow, Trulia, and Yahoo! Real Estate. These sites have become so popular that most MLS now have to post on them. They are the collecting sites for all the listings.

When you post your home on any of these websites, choose the best four to twelve photos. Have that really punchy description of your home and location ready, and include them in your ad.

Don't stop there! Take advantage of Internet networking and use this little ad package to create a personal media blast.

Post an announcement on Facebook, Instagram, or Twitter with a link to your listing so people can see photos and read the details. Tell the world.

Remember to email your information to everyone in your address book, and ask people to pass the word along if they know anyone who's looking to buy a home. Just a few sentences will do it. Try:

Dear Friend,

We have decided to put our house on the market. We have loved living here. If you know of anyone who is looking for a house, please forward this email.

Thanks, (your name)

All of these features are available to work with on the *ListingDoor.com* web application.

You'd be amazed at what a little personal networking can do. I continue to be surprised by how many homes I sell this way. As new media expands people's social networks, it will be more and more likely that one of your friends will know someone who's looking, and they'll pass along that listing on, with a good word about you in the bargain.

There was a time I would've told you that you needed to put your home on MLS but these days it is by no means required. Of course, you *can* also list your home on MLS if you wish. There are companies that will do it for a flat fee, usually around $100 to $200. But be aware that when you list on MLS, you'll be marketing your home to real estate agents that will require you to commit to paying a buyer's agent commission before they will show your listing. If you decide to go this route, you will still need to do everything in this book to ensure you have a first class marketing package like that offered with *ListingDoor.com.*

Even so, it will still be a better deal than paying your own agent, and your calculations will show that it's worthwhile. But dealing with an agent means sacrificing a lot of flexibility so unless it's a tremendously good deal, avoid the industry standards. You now have a choice.

If you are considering the MLS, wait a couple of months before deciding. If you do decide to list your home with them, be sure that you quote all agents and the public the same commission rate. If they do not have an agent, tell them they can deduct the commission. You know your circumstances and home better than anyone.

FACT: *Zillow and Trulia have become the central collecting and posting sites for real estate.*

Here's an insider's tip for when you're ready to pull the trigger: list your home early on a Thursday morning. Active buyers usually dedicate their weekends to the hunt and the homes that catch their eye on Thursday are going to be at the top of their list as well as at the front of their minds! Your home will also have a certain allure if buyers know it was just listed. They'll want to see it before anyone else does.

So I can't use cardboard and markers for my yard sign?

Let's talk about your yard sign. Traditionally, yard signs promote a real estate broker but tell you nothing about the house. The big, fat name of the brokerage firm is all potential buyers have to go on. When a buyer driving by calls the phone number on the sign, they get someone sitting at a marketing desk—not you, the person who's really interested in selling the home!

As we've mentioned before, in most agencies, an agent is required to take a turn answering phones—often without pay—so agencies don't have to pay someone to answer phones full-time. As a result, the potential buyer ends up talking to an agent who probably hasn't even set foot on the property the buyer is asking about. Because the agent knows that answering phone calls is unlikely to lead to an actual deal, he might sound pushy and bored—which is not what you want your buyers to hear.

Don't put up a sign that directs potential buyers to a number answered by *that guy*. Instead, use a personalized yard sign to catch their eye and set the tone for a great transaction.

While most buyers now begin their real estate search on the Internet, they still drive by and explore the neighborhoods they're interested in. The first thing they'll see about your home is your FOR SALE sign—so your sign is important.

A customized sign will advertise your home rather than the name of a big real estate company. When your sign catches their eye and motivates them to call the number listed, they'll speak to you—getting signs of intelligent life rather than a nameless, bored voice at a property desk.

FACT: *A customized yard sign is well worth the cost.*

Skip the generic red and white sign from the hardware store that screams, "I'm desperate to sell my home as quickly as possible, so come take advantage of me." Visuals matter, and it's hard to correct a negative first impression. Create a sign that reflects the value of your home and gives detailed, personalized information. *ListingDoor.com* has great examples of easy–to–make signs that you create yourself right on the site. The custom sign—designed by you—is for you to pick up at your local FedEx, ready to place on the lawn and make it official.

First, however, you need to make up the fact sheet that will give your buyer all the motivation to actually make a call and visit your home. It's crucial, and whether it's only on the fact sheet or posted on a custom sign, it must include this: For Sale by the homeowner, the price, the location/address, number of bedrooms, number of baths, and best features (which could include updates, remodeling, school district, pool, square footage, lot size, etc.) Don't forget to include your contact information.

The first week that your sign goes up, you're probably going to get calls from neighbors about your asking price. This is normal. Don't take offense to it, because your neighbors do have a reasonable, vested interest in knowing. Think about how you've recently researched home prices yourself and politely give them the information. They might also find you a buyer.

Don't get discouraged if your first few calls are dead ends like this. Putting the sign out front is a huge step.

The magic of an open house

Open houses can be very effective in bringing more potential buyers to your home. A lot of people like open houses because they can remain relatively anonymous and see the home without any pressure to interact with the seller.

The hard part about open houses is that you get a lot of window shoppers; inevitably, a sizable part of the crowd will be people just looking for building and decorating ideas or idly comparison shopping.

Open houses are on their way to becoming obsolete anyway because of the Internet searches people can do now. Real estate agents keep them alive as a way to give out their card to new potential clients as well as justify their commissions.

Open houses *do* get people in your house—so by all means, host an open house. Be sure to post a sign out front a week ahead of the event that says, "Open house on Sunday afternoon from 3 to 5." Personally, I prefer an open house between the hours of three and five. Most open houses close at 4 o'clock so a 5 o'clock closing will give you another hour to welcome potential buyers. Choosing to host a slightly later time slot might mean buyers don't have to choose between your house and another one; when four o'clock rolls around, people will come to you.

Open houses save time for you and create a sense of urgency for buyers. When you have three or four people call on Friday and want to come see the house, you tell them to drop by on Sunday when the house will be open. They'll arrive to a house full of other people walking around asking questions, which makes your home seem very much in demand. The imagined competition tends to prompt quick offers from buyers.

Here's a final tip: act like a retail store and capitalize on someone else's foot traffic. If you learn that a real estate firm is having some open houses in your area, try to piggyback onto them and hold your open house the same day. There will be a lot of traffic coming through, so be smart and use it to your advantage.

No one is available to field your call at this time ...

Be prepared to deal with buyers over the phone directly. Welcome calls when they come in and don't let them go to voicemail if you can avoid it. Most buyers will have done their research over the Internet by the time they call and will have a real interest in seeing and buying the home. Being able to deal personally with potential buyers is one of the biggest pluses of being an independent seller so use it to your advantage.

When buyers call, they may be literally outside your house reading your phone number off the sign. And they want answers! They've been conditioned by the Internet to get them. They're going to be frustrated if their call doesn't net them more information and they may not call again.

> **FACT:** *You and your home need to be accessible to your buyers.*

Of course, you have a life. You probably work and can't take calls all the time. You can work around this by using an answering service or by leaving an informative message on your voice mail like this:

> *"Hi, you've reached 713-555-5555. If you're calling about our home for sale at 100 Oak Lane, it's listed for ($ price), and we would love to show it to you. It's spacious, beautiful, on a large lot, and it was recently updated. Please leave your name*

and phone number and I'll call you back as soon as possible."

Real estate agents rarely put the price on flyers or phone messages because they know that if the potential buyer can't afford your home they can show them something else. That's not the case here. It's to your advantage to let the buyer know the price right away.

When you do receive a call from a buyer, write down their name and phone number as soon as you hear it. They may miss an appointment and be too embarrassed to call again, or they may lose your number. You want to be able to call them back instead of waiting for them to call you.

If you're comfortable with the idea, you can consider putting a key lockbox on your home so potential buyers can see it when you can't be there. Just get your valuables out of plain sight and know that real estate agents do this all the time. Remind your potential buyers to lock up after themselves and return the key to the lock box.

There have been recent headlines about how unsafe Open Houses can be.

I like "for sale by owner" because when your home is listed with a firm, there are zero safety precautions in which they are letting buyers into your home. Nothing is 100% foolproof, but here are a few tips; when someone is making an appointment, tell them that for safety purposes you require an email address/cell phone number. At my company, I confirm every appointment with a text and an email. You can take it a step further and ask them to take a picture of their driver's license and text it to you.

This is one area that I think needs serious improvement. As a broker, I am still shocked that firms do not have some form of security in place for both the homeowners and agents.

It's really helpful when inventory is high because you want to provide a convenient way for buyers to see your home whenever possible. A lockbox also allows second–time viewers to take their time in a no–pressure environment and decide whether your home is right for them.

I had a lockbox when I was selling my own home. I kept the lights on during the day so it was always ready. I wanted all the showings I could get!

Bottom Lines:

1. If this sounds like a lot of work, remember this: You would be providing most of the same information to a real estate agent, and you're being well paid for your effort—because you get to keep the commission.
2. You can use ads, Internet networking, and yard signs to pull people in.
3. An open house may generate interested buyers and will create a sense that your house is in demand.
4. Be prompt and polite when dealing with the public.

"Companion Workbook" Download
http://po.st/workbook22

Chapter 7

WHAT SHOULD I DO WHILE I WAIT FOR THE PHONE TO RING?

People usually look at a lot of places when they are looking for a home to buy. They end up nicknaming them: the "House Near the Gas Station" or the "House with the Green Awning and the Nice Skylight", etc.

My friend bought a house she and her husband privately called the "House that Landscaping Forgot." The house had many attractive features, but they always remembered it as the only place they saw where the front lawn ran right up to the front wall of the house, uninterrupted by bushes or flowers or *anything*.

For a few hundred dollars or less, the owners could have put in a few flowering shrubs, edging rocks and a little mulch so potential buyers would remember it as the "House with the Great Hardwood Floors" instead of the "House that Landscaping Forgot."

A little bit of sprucing up goes a long way toward making a house memorable for the *right* reasons.

People will remember a house that makes them feel good. They'll also remember a house that depresses them, but they will buy the one that makes them feel good. Spending $200 on landscaping can easily get you another $10,000 in the price.

There are a lot of great TV shows now about "staging," the act of dressing up your house to look its best. Go to HGTV.com Home Staging [http://po.st/simplesold29] and watch some of the impressive transformations they've done. ListingDoor's Pinterest [http://po.st/simplesold30] and Houzz [http://po.st/simplesold31] are two other great sites. You can hire professionals to do this kind of work, but if you watch a couple TV shows you'll be able to do almost as good a job yourself.

FACT: *Staging can be a lot of fun!*

People like color so make sure they see color as they approach the house. Flowers are inexpensive and can make a huge difference in the look of a home's exterior.

For the inside of the house, the best mood is "bright and clean." Start with bright. Nothing is as depressing as a dim, drab-looking room—so brighten it up. Paint the walls a lighter shade if you have to. Buy more lamps and turn them on. Buyers will choose the house that makes them feel the right emotion, and bright is a happy emotion.

Clean and bright go hand in hand. I recently sold a property that sat on the market for a long time because even though the house was structurally sound, it was just plain gloomy inside. Dark brown paneling made every room seem small, depressing and … dirty. The baby blue carpeting was stained with twenty-five years of living. People would walk in and say, "this place needs too much work." It was a fine house, but the dreary atmosphere made it look like a teardown.

We had the walls painted a neutral shade of white and replaced the flooring with new, seagrass carpeting. The paint job was $2,000, but it completely changed the impression the house made. Everyone who saw it after that commented on how utterly changed it was, and the eventual selling more than made up for the investment in paint and carpeting.

FACT: *Neutral colors are always your best bet.*

Maybe you can't afford $2,000 to repaint your walls—but you can afford to keep your house clean. You want your buyer to focus on what's important—the message that your home is right for them. You don't want them distracted by any obvious flaws. A greasy pan in the kitchen sink might not affect the value of your house, but it will affect the impression your house makes—and you only get one chance to make a good first impression.

A few easy corrections will help you achieve an outstanding look and feel to your home and help you get top dollar. At this stage, you're still telling your house's story and housekeeping is part of it.

Consult this checklist before showing your house

Remember how you had to clean up your house before you took those photographs? Now you have to do most of it again—but instead of moving the cat litter box for the photograph and moving it right back again, you have to find a more permanent place (like the garage) to stash it between uses.

You must depersonalize the house. All the touches that make your house feel cozy to you represent *you.* A potential buyer has to be able to imagine himself or herself living there, and that's hard to do if there's a photo of your favorite politician on the wall.

Speaking of pictures, we have a problem here in Texas. Everybody has a picture of themselves posing with one of the former presidents. Even if that shot of you and George W. is your prized possession, take it down before you show the house. You don't want anybody's political biases to emerge if they are going to interfere with a speedy home sale!

I have a friend who knows country singer George Strait. She proudly displays a picture of herself and Mr. Strait—but I advised her to take it down when showing her house. "It's better not to show George Strait at all unless he comes with the house," I said.

Below are steps to take to get ready for your first home viewers.

1. Clean up all clutter. It is the most important thing you can do.
2. Keep the rooms clean, light, and bright. Open the drapes, turn on the lamps, and make sure all bulbs are working. Clear ceiling fixtures of all the dead insects that always seem to find their way inside. You might not notice their little silhouettes anymore but a potential buyer will.
3. Put away all personal items and toiletries in your bathroom.
4. Take everything off the kitchen counters, pull the magnets off your fridge, and hide the pet bowls. Don't have pets in the house if you can possibly avoid it.
5. Tidy up the exterior again. Trim the bushes, mow the lawn and blow away the leaves. Put away all hoses, trash cans and recycling. Hide the sign for the security company.
6. Clean up the pool if you have one.
7. Make sure there are no toys lying around, inside or out.
8. Stash sports and fitness equipment in the garage.
9. Put away anything that is too personal. Slide photos into a drawer and get your mail off the coffee table.

If you really hate to clean or really have no time to do it, find a good housecleaning service on Craigslist or Google by your zip code and hire them do the major work. The expense will more than pay off by making your house look more desirable.

You might as well fix it now

Let's talk about deferred maintenance, like the broken window that you always meant to replace or the torn–up screen door. Such minor repairs will need to be fixed once and for all. And don't limit your inventory to only what's obvious. If your kitchen is a faded shade of taupe from the early '90s, it would look a lot better with a new color on the walls.

Replace worn out carpet or get it shampooed. Touch up hardwood floors. If your tub is chipped, re–glaze it.

You may not feel like making any additional expenditures, but don't assume buyers won't take your fresh–looking kitchen into account as they picture themselves in your home. Especially don't make the mistake of thinking that buyers will overlook minor repairs that need to be made!

Obvious signs of wear and tear will tell them that you haven't taken care of your home. You've already told them how much you love your home and how happy you've been there. Flaws will put a crack in this story and make the whole thing seem unreliable.

Take a tour of your home as if you were a picky potential buyer and act accordingly. Small flaws can seem fatal in the current market. A dirty rug can take $5,000 off your home's selling price. I've seen it happen.

You don't need to fix everything before you start showing it, but it's a smart idea to go ahead and take care of the things that stand out. Remember, you will make more money if you get these repairs done before you negotiate. Buyers will pay closer to the asking price if your home already shows a complete package of what they want—not a house that will need some immediate fixing-up.

I always advise sellers to get a fresh coat of paint or at least touch up the current one. It always pays off by making the home look newer—for the low, low price of a couple cans of paint.

The cost of painting yourself or even hiring someone to do the job is a lot less expensive than negotiating with a buyer on a painting allowance. If you end up negotiating, the buyer will always want to price the allowance according to the most expensive brand of paint and the most expensive painting service.

Choose your improvements wisely

Are you thinking about doing some more serious pre-show remodeling? Maybe you feel that your home can't compete because you haven't updated. You're right to realize the value of making your home a more attractive prospect, but be sure to spend your money wisely.

Shoot for a neutral, up-to-date esthetic in any improvements. You don't know who your buyers are going to be or what kind of decorating taste they'll have. Remember that if they do buy, they probably aren't going to have a ton of cash lying around to replace anything they don't like, and will have to live with it until they can afford to replace it. Be careful not to do anything they might not like, like repainting in a questionable color scheme.

Go for it if there's a room in your home that could use a good remodeling. I knew of a one-bedroom apartment in New York City that initially listed for $310,000 (a price that makes me grateful that I live in Texas). Then the seller decided to replace the kitchen cabinets, prompting the real estate agent to put it back on the market for $429,000. Eventually, it sold for $417,000 —$107,000 more than the original asking price and much more than the seller paid for the new cabinets. This is serious money.

We say we don't judge books by their covers—but we really do.

Will people actually notice whether I've mowed?

You made everything look as clean and beautiful as possible when you took pictures of the outside of your house for marketing. Minor repairs outside are just as important as minor repairs inside.

Buyers are much more likely to start a serious inquiry when they drive by a home and see something gorgeous. That's why drive-bys are so important. Research starts on the web but ends on the ground. More than half the calls I get are from buyers prompted by an attractive drive-by.

Go outside and look at your home with a buyer's eyes. Is the yard nicely landscaped and well maintained? Are the plantings lush and trimmed? Apply fertilizer or add grass if it's winter. In summer, remember that grass can grows very quickly and should be mowed at least once per week.

Remove clutter from the yard and clean the gutters. Trim down or remove dead bushes. Repaint the front door and put a pot of flowers at the entrance as an easy, personal touch.

Think of the sprucing-up as a project in itself. It is an important part of the larger process of selling your own home.

Power wash the sidewalk or driveway if you have to. Fix doorknobs that jiggle or stick. Is the front entrance a true reflection of the quality of your home? Be sure the front door and the first few steps you take inside give visitors the feeling that they're entering a warm, inviting space.

Do whatever is necessary to create a homey feeling, starting with the outer layer. Most people do their drive-bys after work so keep exterior and interior lights on in the evening. Spread some mulch, but put gardening tools or ladders away when you're done. Make sure fences and gates are repaired. Sweep the corners of the front porch.

You and I know that these superficial aspects aren't really relevant to the prospective buyer's experience inside the home, but such appearance-driven details help create a positive emotional picture that goes a long way.

Remember, cleaning up your property doesn't need to be emotional. Be objective as you evaluate changes that need to be made. Take all personal feelings about the home out of the picture.

Little things mean a lot

There are a few remaining small touches that make a big difference in the atmosphere of your home and how it affects buyers.

1) **Scents and aromas.** Don't burn scented candles! Men generally hate them, and many people are allergic to strong scents. The convention of having a cloying, berry-vanilla fragrance waft through an open house is just a marketing ploy by the candle makers. Forget aromatherapy oils, too. Your house should just smell clean. All you need to do before a showing is wipe the counters with a subtle pine cleanser. That's the only fragrance you'll need.
2) **Hobbies.** Store away all collections and memorabilia. Charming though they may be, it's harder for any buyers to imagine their futures if your hobbies and affiliations are everywhere.
3) **Valuables.** Do not leave valuables out and visible. Rent a safe deposit box if you have anything of real value that you want to safeguard. Remember to put your jewelry back on before

a showing. Clients sometimes inadvertently leave a wedding ring or watch sitting on the sink after a quick cleanup.

4) **Pets.** I have dogs, and I love them, but they're animals, and they smell like animals. Be sure your home is free of any lingering pet odors. Pick up the dog poop in the backyard. A family looking at the house is going to walk around the back yard and no one wants to step in a dog poop landmine! If you can, stash the dog at a friend's house or put them in a crate before visitors arrive. A lot of people are afraid of dogs. A pet cat will probably hide during a home showing, but the litter box should be out of sight or out in the garage until the guests leave.
5) **Fireplaces.** Clean the fireplace and clear all clutter from the mantel. Too many knickknacks are never a good look, and the buyer will likely remember the knickknacks instead of the beautiful fireplace.
6) **Personal statements.** Remove anything that could make a buyer feel uncomfortable, including anything religious or that might be considered controversial. Put away the old Playboy magazines, even if they are collectors' items. Take any deer trophies or animal heads down from the walls. You don't want to lose a great buyer because their kids screamed when they saw Bambi on the wall. Your home has to be acceptable to all buyers—not just hunters. Make it easier for them to picture themselves in the home by making it as neutral as possible.
7) **Bright colors.** Repaint strong/intense colors with neutral shades if you can. Sellers hate to hear this, but I can assure you that the brightly painted room is the one thing buyers

always remember. And that will be its nickname, the "One with the Bright Red Room." It's the home you're trying to showcase, not your own personal esthetic.

8) **Windows.** Wipe window sills clean and always have drapes and blinds open unless there is an undesirable view. Switch the lights on in every room during showings.
9) **Bathrooms.** Always do a quick run-through and check your bathrooms. Toilet seats should be down. Buy a new bath mat and bath towels, and don't use the towels. These are just for show! Buy a new shower curtain and rings. Glass shower doors should be crystal clear and free of soap scum
10) **Sound effects.** Don't leave the TV or music on; it's too distracting. You might like country music, but what if your potential buyer loathes it? Don't take that chance.
11) **Special stories.** If you are leaving any special light fixtures, put the backstory on a card. People love stories!
12) **Warnings**. Post a small sign near steep attic or basement stairs warning visitors to watch their step.
13) **Behind closed doors.** Remember, buyers are nosey! They love to look in cabinets, drawers, and closets. They probably won't rummage around, but they will see anything lying on top when they first open a drawer. My client once opened a kitchen drawer and saw an IRS lien letter. What do you think that said to this potential buyer?
14) **Street numbers.** Have your address clearly visible from the street—as in, HUGE! Make it memorable and easy to find.
15) **Information packages.** Gather your warranties, plans and operating manuals and put them in a folder when you're getting your house ready to sell. Prospective buyers might

want to know these details, and it's nice to have it ready to hand over at closing. Buyers will also ask about utility bills so put those in a folder, too, just in case.

16) **Temperature.** Err on the side of excess when setting air conditioning or heating for showings. The house should be slightly cooler or warmer than adequate. Show that your A/C and heating systems work.
17) **Welcome.** Finally, buy a new welcome mat. This is the first thing people see when entering. Nothing is sweeter than a big welcome to someone's new home!

The laundry basket cleanup trick

Clutter is one of the most important but most overlooked factors influencing whether or not you get your asking price. Buyers think clutter is contagious for some reason! Too much stuff around makes them doubt their stuff will fit.

Clutter has been known to take off 5 to 15 percent off the asking price because buyers are less inclined to make a high offer for a house that looks messy. In early 2011, two identical apartments in New York City went on sale at exactly the same time; one was cluttered, and the other had been cleared out. The clean one sold quickly. The messy one languished on the market for a year and sold for 15 percent less than the clean one.

Trust me, this applies to any house in any town. Having clutter is like having a strip club across the street. No one will want to live there!

Clutter takes a while to accumulate, and it takes a while to clear it out. Take advantage of the opportunity to purge your home of stuff you don't need and save the cost of moving it to your new place. I had a client who ordered a POD, filled it with his clutter then had it carted away—just to clear it away as quickly as possible. Take those big measures and get rid of extraneous things.

You can make some money while you're at it, on sites like eBay or Craigslist. After all, one man's trash is another man's treasure. You can also donate excess things. A good de–cluttering strategy for kids whose rooms look like the toy section of Walmart is to let them keep their 10 favorite toys, and then give to kids who don't have any toys. It's also a valuable life lesson.

Non–essential stuff you want to keep can go into storage. Free up an over–crowded room by putting a chair or two in storage. Buyers will see more space and be willing to pay for it. People believe organization is contagious, too! If you have a spacious and perfectly organized home, they'll think they will live in a perfectly organized home, too once they move in.

There's nothing more important than keeping your home immaculately clean for potential buyers when the time comes to start showing it. However, you're still going to be living there during this process, and life is messy. Rather than walk on eggshells until it sells, use a tried and true trick: the "laundry basket cleanup."

This is where you turn in those inevitable moments when you've spread all your papers for something out on the table, or your kids have made a huge mess, or some domestic accident has occurred—and you get a call from a potential buyer who wants to stop by in five minutes.

FACT: *You need to be prepared to clean FAST!*

All you need to do when those moments arise is keep an empty laundry basket handy, scoop all the clutter into it and stow it in the backseat of the car. When the coast is clear, you can get right back to what you were doing. Until next time.

Be sure to put the mail in the laundry basket, too. You don't want anyone to see important papers or start thinking about bills when they see your house. I can't tell you how many times I've shown a house with mortgage delinquency notices sitting right out in the open for all the world to see. Don't let your stock market accounts be visible, either. You don't want your personal finances to enter into the negotiation. Buyers should see only what you want them to see.

Even if finances are tight and you can't do any extensive repairs or renovations, your house can still look neat and clean—it's the most important thing to be done to prepare for showings. Martha Stewart has a great spring cleaning checklist on her website—you might want to check it out. I'm a big believer in learning from the best, and she's definitely the best when it comes to obsessive cleaning. So no matter what season it is, it's time for you to spring clean!

Neatly stack all the contents of your cabinets, especially the pantry and bathroom cabinets, because viewers are definitely going to open them for a look. Full closets look tiny, so clear them out. All closets should contain the minimum, even children's closets, and be organized neatly. Buyers notice messes, even when they are a child's fault. Even cute clutter is unattractive.

Do not forget the garage. You may think of the garage as a place to store Christmas lights and bicycles, and it might not matter much to you. But many men buy a house because of the garage. Do your best to make it look like a usable space.

Start now to think about the garage and all other storage areas in terms of the upcoming move. It's all going to have to be sorted and packed or tossed, no matter what. Get the worst of it over now.

If I sound like a neat freak, just trust my experience. Clutter counts.

Um, so, this is the living room

You want to show your house like a professional, so act professional. And start at the very beginning of the process.

Give potential buyers good directions to your house. People get lost, even when using a GPS. Out–of–town buyers in particular will wander around driving in circles until they get frustrated and leave. A frustrating trip to the house sets a bad tone for the showing. Nip this problem in the bud by having clear, easy–to–follow directions that include obvious landmarks.

Have a fact sheet ready to give potential buyers so they won't have to call you back for important details like lot size or the size of the master bedroom.

Prospective buyers are going to ask why you're moving and leaving the house. Prepare the right answer so you're not caught off guard. You could be downsizing because the children are grown. Maybe your family is growing, and you need a larger place or maybe your spouse wants to be closer to work.

Don't say things like, "well, we don't like what's happened to the neighborhood" or "there's too much traffic." Don't shoot yourself in the foot by blurting out any honest misgivings you have about the house. Think ahead about the impact of your answer.

Everything you say during showings should make your buyers want to move farther along in the process. Your house should be able to sell itself by this point, as long as you don't bad–mouth it.

Keep chatter to a polite minimum during a showing. Allow buyers to roam through the house freely and don't hover. When they arrive, ask something like this: "would you like me to show you the house, or would you rather walk through by yourself?" They'll usually ask for a tour so you can point out details, but your question will show that you trust them and are ready for the home to be theirs.

Remember, the buyer will recognize the kitchen as a kitchen, so don't feel you have to introduce it. Don't talk their ear off just to fill the void. Save your words to sell them on the neighborhood and the neighbors.

Instead of saying something like, "Yep, well, this is the dining room..." say instead, "This dining room is great for a big Christmas dinner because everybody can fit comfortably at the table for hours and visit...." Or, "We love the living room because it overlooks the yard. It's so nice to sit on the couch and read with the doors open and cool summer breeze wafting in." Leave it at that! A few sentences are enough. You don't want to be pushy.

Then, after you have walked a buyer through the home, say something like, "I know this is a lot to take in. I'm going to step outside and let you walk through on your own. Please take your time." Being gracious goes a long way. Give them an hour to wander around.

If a buyer wishes to come back a second time, leave them alone but offer to be available for questions. Give them the freedom to walk around and decide if this is the new home they are looking for. Your buyers will appreciate this immensely.

Finally, don't be discouraged if you gear up to show your house and it takes a while to get the first showing. Homes were shown up to four times a week during the "go–go" days of the real estate boom, but we're not in that type of market now. Don't panic if you end up showing your home only a few times a month. Concentrate on making each showing as effective as possible.

Bottom Lines:

1. Put some work into getting the house visitor–ready.
2. Make important repairs inside and out, and take the opportunity to get rid of clutter.
3. "Stage" the house so it looks its best.
4. Be professional and gracious with potential buyers—and don't talk too much.

"Companion Workbook" Download
http://po.st/workbook22

Chapter 8

A BUYER SEEMS INTERESTED! NOW WHAT?

Sarah was showing her house to potential buyers—Marci and Ned—one bright Saturday morning. After a brief tour, she took a seat on the front porch and let them wander from room to room, exploring.

Marci was impressed with the kitchen and opened the cabinets twice. Her husband spent half an hour measuring space in the garage. They were both smiling every time Sarah peeked in.

Finally, they approached her. "We like this place," Marci said.

"You know, we've been looking at other houses in this area, but that gorgeous old chandelier in the dining room really makes this one stand out," Ned added.

Marci nodded enthusiastically. "I can just picture serving Thanksgiving dinner on our oak dining table under the chandelier."

It sounded like they were going to make an offer—but Sarah didn't feel much like celebrating because of the sinking feeling in her stomach. The chandelier had deep sentimental value to her, and she was planning to take it with her when she moved.

Your buyers should already know in advance which wonderful items in the house you're selling and which are not for sale and will be coming with you. A family heirloom that is leaving when you leave should be clearly specified in the brochure you give prospective buyers.

Things that you need to keep in your home to show it but that you'll take when you leave are called "exclusions." Those include anything attached or built–in to the home like special light fixtures, fountains, stereo equipment, and some appliances. That means you can't be too attached to anything that's attached to the house.

Exclusions can become a source of conflict between you and the buyer if you don't disclose all the necessary information beforehand. Remember, your relationship with the buyer is crucial: clarity builds trust.

I can't stress this enough. I have seen many a deal implode over a small exclusion.

Never start negotiating price or finalizing a contract with a buyer until you have pinned down what you are going to take with you. You have to head off any unnecessary problems before you get to the crucial negotiation stage.

But my *grandmother* gave me that!

Exclusions should always be listed on the brochure that you give potential buyers who come to tour your home.

So what to include as an exclusion? If you have a real statement piece in your house—something that gives character to an entire room, like a huge, nailed–in, wall–to–wall bookcase—and you're not including it in the sale, it's an exclusion.

Whatever is attached to the house is assumed to be part of the package and expected to stay with the home. If you're showing something but intend to keep it, list it as an exclusion on the brochure. Better yet, remove it if possible and replace it with something else before you show the house.

People are interested in your house because they like the *whole look* of it. Maintaining that look can sometimes make or break a sale, so don't hand the buyer a marketing brochure that's mostly exclusions. A long, long list of the nice things on display that you'll be taking with you might make buyers feel like they're getting taken.

Think about how you feel when you go to buy a car. What if, as soon as you showed interest, they started switching the leather seats for cloth and telling you that all the car's best features were just for show? Salespeople call that "bait and switch"— the customer is lured in by attractive bait, but a switch is made at the last moment.

You have *too many* exclusions if you're running into multiple items on a long list in your marketing brochure of things in your house that you want to keep. It's best to remove and replace a few of them before you start showing the house.

If something is attached to the house and you're not die–hard emotionally attached to *it*, just let it go. List it in the marketing brochure as something that is staying with the house.

You won't save money by taking the light fixtures, because knowing that he or she will have to purchase new ones, the buyer is going to negotiate the price down. And the buyer is not going to like the hassle involved. Only keep an item if it's irreplaceable and you're emotionally connected to it. In most cases, ceiling fans and light fixtures don't fall into this category. I almost had a sale fall apart over a built–in backyard playset!

FACT: *Exclusions may seem trivial, but they can spark contract-cancelling disputes.*

I cannot tell you how many deals fall apart over something as trivial as the chandelier in the dining room, which would have been a non–issue if the seller had been up front about having inherited the chandelier from his grandmother and couldn't bear to let it go. In cases like this, it's not really about the light fixture; it's about hurt feelings. Both parties get offended over what they perceive as a lack of honesty and greediness on both sides when, in reality, the only thing that went wrong was non–disclosure.

If, for some reason, you really can't replace your exclusions, do your best to explain to potential buyers why you want to keep them. For example, maybe you and your husband bought those fireplace sconces on your honeymoon. Sentimental reasons go over much better than just "I don't want to buy new light fixtures." People are usually respectful of and sympathetic to personal reasons.

When they seem to love your things as much as your house

What appliances are included in the sale? There are some traditional considerations here of which you might not be aware. Built–in refrigerators and microwaves generally stay with the home. Washers and dryers usually go with the seller—but you must make it clear that you *are* planning to take the washer and dryer with you. They can always be negotiated. Ceiling fans usually stay.

Drapes are tricky. If they match your bedspread and you absolutely must take them, explain it. If you can leave them, leave them. Buyers usually don't like moving into a completely stripped house knowing they can't actually spend the night there until there's *something* covering the bedroom windows. This is especially true if they loved the way that it looked when they first saw it.

The framed mirrors above the powder room sink will be assumed to stay, even if they're not "built in" to the wall. You have to list them as exclusions if you plan to take them with you.

Then there are the television, phone system, and surround–sound system. Flat screens are often attached to walls and therefore technically a part of the house you're selling. You'll probably want to take your TV but if you were planning to upgrade to a larger screen anyway, use the built–in flat screen as a selling point for the house. Otherwise, list it as an exclusion to avoid a gray area.

Some clients will love your things as much or more than they love the house. I once represented a buyer who thought *everything* should stay with the home; I think she would have asked for the seller's portrait above the fireplace if she could have! I was embarrassed by her behavior even though she was a client. We finally got the list of exclusions on the third visit—much later in the game than is preferable. Avoid any haggling with a buyer by making it clear beforehand what you are willing to part with.

FACT: *Exclusions are often negotiable.*

You have the option of making your exclusions negotiable. Even if you like a furnishing/fixture, as long as you know you can buy another one, let it go—and buy another one for your new home. You might want to keep the antique bathroom mirror—but you *could* replace it. If keeping the mirror tips your buyer into closing the deal, letting it go may be well worthwhile.

You never know what your buyer will want you to leave or what they might insist that you take. A play set in the backyard could be the cherry on top of the perfect house to one family; to another family with grown children, the play set could be a nuisance that will need to be removed (and probably by you at your expense) before they'll consider making an offer.

All this can be worked out but don't wait until an item becomes a point of contention before deciding how you feel about it. Moving is a great time to purge, to release the past, and get new stuff, so err on the side of letting things go—as long as the buyer wants them.

Again, do your best to leave your emotions out of it. Of course, you're going to be attached to things in your house. You bought them; you associate them with memories, and you love them. But the ultimate goal is to sell your house. You can replace great curtains, but you can't replace a perfectly timed offer from buyers who are eager to make a deal.

Getting credit for your improvements

Make a specific and detailed list of improvements you have made to the home. Tell potential buyers about the energy-efficient air conditioners you installed (and how much lower your electricity bill has been since you got them). Mention what your new kitchen countertop is made of or what you updated in the bathroom. Buyers love knowing that they're getting something that's almost new.

If you've done a major remodeling, let buyers know the approximate cost and which contractors you used. Prove how you have made your home significantly and tangibly more valuable. Buyers appreciate details.

An important note: we live in litigious times where anyone threatens to sue over anything. Do your best to be accurate when describing improvements, but always use the word "approximately" when referring to how old something is. For example, "the roof is *approximately* five years old."

If the offer is insultingly low, do I still have to be polite?

You should end up with a contract that's pretty close to your asking price if you've done your homework and priced your home on the market. But don't be insulted if an offer comes in lower than the asking price.

Whether it's for a car or home or anything else, we've all tried to grab a significant bargain in our life. That's the way of the world now. Don't take it personal.

To begin with, a buyer should not be allowed to deduct the would–be agent's commission because you are selling your home yourself, even if their instinct tells them that would be fair. Let the buyer know that you've done all the work the real estate agent would do and more. Keeping the commission and being in control are the biggest perks of selling your home on your own, so don't make that negotiable.

You can try to get a buyer's lowball offer increased. First, always send back a gracious response, even if the buyer is offering you 50 percent of your asking price. Then try to switch to a positive mindset. Be flattered that someone wrote an offer for the house, not upset about the "amount" they didn't offer. Kindness allows you to be firm as you explain why your asking price is what it is.

FACT: *You should be flattered by every offer—and you should counter every offer too.*

That's right, it's a good idea to counter all offers, no matter what they are. Both parties are trying to get the best bargain possible, and you both have the right to express what price works for you.

Unfortunately, there's a tendency these days to focus only on the "SQ. FT.," the price per square foot and I have a hard time with this. Just because two homes are the same size doesn't mean they should be priced equally; quality comes into the equation. One house might be beautifully done, with exquisite, top–quality construction; another house might be cheaply built with no trim. One house might have cost less than $110 a square foot to build while another might have cost $350. These homes *shouldn't* have a comparable "square footage" price. That would be like comparing a stripped Suburban to a Denali in terms of cost per square inch.

If your buyer tries to lower his price by comparing the price per square foot, draw his or her attention to the aspects of your home that justify your price. Go through the comparable home sales that you found in your research. If your home has recent updates or refurbishments, explain how those things are factored in.

Maybe your lot is bigger than other houses with comparable square footage. Maybe you've updated your home recently. Maybe your price is already lower than average because you *haven't* updated your home. Maybe you live on a corner and have two big, gorgeous windows looking out onto the street.

Respond to the buyer in detail and in writing. Show that your asking price is fair and well–thought–out. Show that you're not keeping any secrets—that you're aware of the market and that your home truly is a good option for them.

You're still marketing at this stage, so I'd advise with a story that illustrates why your home is worth your asking price. I had a client in Houston who was trying to sell his home in St. Louis. He called me and said, "Gosh, we've got an offer, but it's way too low, and we just can't get this buyer to raise it. What do you think we should do?"

I asked him, "Well, why did you buy that house?"

"Oh, it's an old dairy farm, and we just loved that," he said. "It's like a place you'd go on a vacation. We never have to give local people the address. You say 'the old dairy farm' and people automatically know where to go."

This great story shows why their home was such a special find. In the letter that my client wrote back to the buyer, he told them what he told me. He said the home was a local landmark, and that its charm and age set it apart from all the new homes in the area.

It was a truly unique house, and by telling its special story, he got the buyer to come up with a satisfactory price.

Eight simple rules for negotiating your price

Read this section carefully. Professionalism and knowledge of the territory will be essential for you at this point in the transaction.

Be aware that the terms and conditions of the contract can make a big difference. At this stage and in this market, "cash is king" more than ever. That means a cash offer goes straight to the front of the line. These offers are worth far more than an offer that is contingent upon a buyer getting financing, which is far more common.

If your offer is contingent on financing, know that your buyer has to start the mortgage process as soon as you agree on the terms of the contract. Each of you has a big, important horse in the race either way. You need to operate in a gracious, efficient, considerate manner in order for negotiations to proceed smoothly from here.

Rule #1: Try to avoid going back and forth more than three times. Generally, each round of negotiations takes on a specific tone, with each round getting more contentious. In the first round, the buyer and seller are thinking about the home. In the second round, they stop thinking about the home and start thinking about the money. In the third round, they start thinking not about the home or money but about the deal itself—and that's when the resentment sets in. After the third round, egos enter the picture, and things get personal. Don't let the negotiations progress to the point where things get personal.

Most people have only a negative experience with negotiations, usually in the context of buying a car. It's likely that your buyer will be predisposed to negativity in the process of working out the contract. In my experience, dealing straightforward and graciously will result in a win/win outcome for buyer and seller. Make all your desired changes on the first contract and fully explain your reasons. Get it all on the table and maintain an attitude of cordial respect.

Rule #2: Stay focused on completing the sale. Never let the buyer's emotions or personality distract you from your goal. Stay calm and gracious, as you would in a business negotiation. You're already at an advantage because you're selling direct and only have two people's agendas to keep in mind—yours and the buyer. You share the same goal. Remember, it's not about winning or losing, but about getting the house sold.

Rule #3: Get everything in writing. Having the buyer put their initial offer in writing ensures that the buyer is serious; having your counteroffer in writing tells the buyer that *you're* serious.

Verbal counteroffers are fraught with potential misunderstandings, misinterpretations, and omissions. If there are only one or two minor changes to be made on the contract, you can negotiate those things verbally and put them in writing later, but all major changes need to be out in writing right away.

I find buyers more willing to accept a counter price when it is submitted in writing, and you will benefit greatly from having your reasons written out for the buyer to see. Every change on a contract needs to be initialed by both the buyer and seller before it goes into escrow.

Rule #4: When you give a concession, ask for something in return, even if it's something small. Buyers can be aggressive in today's market. If you don't assert yourself (in a reasonable way), the buyer might come back and ask for more.

For example, say the buyer wants a certain repair done. If you agree to this, you might ask to close earlier. If you don't agree to make the repair, offer to leave the window treatments instead. Even if you don't get what you ask for, you'll have set the stage for the buyer to make fewer demands.

Rule #5: Keep everything confidential until it closes. Never gloat or talk about your sale in detail with others. You don't want anyone telling your buyer that he or she overpaid, which people love to say regardless of the price.

Worse, talking too much could shut your deal down completely. I knew a seller who went around bragging about the price she got for her home. A neighbor down the street who had been thinking of selling, heard the price and put her place on the market during the option period of the contract.

The buyer of the first house walked out on the earnest money contract, went down the street and bought the home that was priced for a few thousand dollars less! This would never have happened had the original seller kept her mouth zipped. You don't want to learn this lesson the hard way.

Rule #6: When you come across something on the contract that you want to counter, mark it and go back to it. Consider the entire contract before you start countering. You can probably live with the one thing you don't like if the rest of the contract is great.

Rule #7: Avoid the words "no" or "never" which create a negative atmosphere in negotiations. Negative words make buyers think you're shutting the door. Try saying, "that doesn't work for us—but this does."

Rule #8: *Always* counter a contract within twenty–four hours, and preferably within twelve. You want to maintain the enthusiasm in the negotiations. Procrastination is the ultimate deal–killer. After forty–eight hours, an offer is typically null and void in the buyer's mind.

The rule I go by is this: the last person to sign or initial is the person that is responsible for getting the contract to the other party. For example, if you make and initial a change on the contract, then the ball is in your court. You need to inform the buyer what you did when you did it, and when you'll be dropping (or emailing) off the paperwork. Let your buyer know that this is the system you want to operate on and you'll prevent miscommunications—as well as keep the ball rolling.

But I hate to haggle!

Maybe you're the kind of person who isn't comfortable negotiating. There are some people who will walk into a car dealership and drive out with an incredible bargain because they enjoyed taking a tough–as–nails stance and outlasting the salesperson. But maybe you're the kind of person who would rather *eat* nails than have to argue about price.

Remember that you are in charge when you're selling your house. You have something big and valuable to offer, and the only question is how much someone will pay for it.

At this point, if you hate to haggle, you might wish you had an agent to do the negotiating for you. You might think, "They're trained in negotiating, and they're good at it." That's just not true! The art of negotiating is not part of the training a real estate agent takes to get a license. As we've said, agents learn by trial and error, and their "errors" can cost home sellers plenty.

If you had a real estate agent, his or her role at this point would be to carry offers and counter-offers back and forth—nothing else. The offers might not be conveyed in a timely manner, either because the agent has other houses to sell and other things to do.

An agent in the middleman role at this point would not only slow things down, it's very possible that he or she would *not* be working to get you the most possible money, but to get the deal closed at any price and collect the commission.

Right now, you want to get to a point where you and the buyer agree on a price. Use the advantage being a direct seller gives you to get there faster.

You can give the buyer instant, person-to-person feedback. Adapt your strategy to make sure the deal keeps going without major problems. If negotiations seem to shift from price to some other obstacle—like exclusions—you'll hear this from the buyer, and you can address the issue immediately.

An agent might not tell you the buyer is concerned about the backyard, and he might not tell the buyer that you are a gardener who would be more than happy to throw in a few fruit trees to keep the deal moving. Negotiations that pass through another person can lose something in the translation, and what is lost might be the key point that makes or breaks the deal.

When you negotiate face-to-face—in this day and age, it's more likely to be by email, but it's still *person-to-person*—you and the buyer can respond to each other's concerns directly. Your marketing strategy can stay flexible enough to meet the buyer's needs.

Be cooperative and proactive. Be a salesman and advocate for your house. Stay professional and keep your emotions out of it.

If the process gets tiring, remember how much equity you're saving by cutting out the middleman and keep that smile on your face! If you were going through this process with a real estate agent, you'd have the same amount of hassle and you'd be fielding twice as many phone calls.

Bottom Lines:

1. Know exactly what you're selling and what's not included.
2. Be prepared to explain how you arrived at your asking price.
3. Stay professional, unemotional, cordial, and focused.
4. Follow the rules for negotiations.

"Companion Workbook" Download
http://po.st/workbook22

Chapter 9

HOW CAN I TELL WHAT GOES INTO ALL THIS PAPERWORK?

So you and the buyer have agreed upon a price and all the other particulars. Time to break open the champagne? Not just yet. The sale isn't over until you have the money in your hand. I've seen too many cases where the seller loaded up his car and was in the driveway, ready to take off for his new location when the deal came screeching to a halt. It's not an everyday occurrence, but it can happen.

A buyer can still change his mind, no matter how sincere he seems. Or his bank can change its mind. In 2008, lenders canceled thousands of mortgages that were in progress. Or some missing bit of paperwork can cause an unforeseen delay.

So don't start loading the moving van until you know the deal is a *done* deal.

So very many sheets of paper

Do you remember getting writer's cramp the day you bought your house? Do you remember having to sign your name what seemed like hundreds of times? This might give you the idea that the housing contract is an unbelievably complex document that's as thick as a big-city phone book.

This transaction won't be as complex. Remember, you were

borrowing money from a bank when you bought your house; lenders have documents to protect them from every possible situation that could occur. Most of the pages in that mountain of paperwork were the lending documents, but those are only a factor when you *buy* a home—not when you sell. That pile of documents goes *way down* when the bank is being paid back its money; they make it easy for you!

In fact, many of the sheets of paper you had to sign with the earnest money were from the real estate agency, absolving them of liability of one kind or another. Your signature was promising them again and again that you wouldn't hold them responsible if something went wrong.

When you work without an agent or agency, the pile of paperwork is much smaller and more manageable. And most of it is boilerplate—standard wording that is used over and over on everybody's contracts.

The buyer is responsible for writing the contract. You don't make it up from scratch. Writing the contract is not a difficult process. These days, contracts are fill–in–the–blank. But it will be much to your benefit if you know what the various parts of the contract entail.

The *ListingDoor.com* website has a useful worksheet that will help you extract the important parts of the contract from jargon that might be confusing. This will be critical when you counter the contract, and it will come in handy if you receive offers from two separate buyers.

Remember to compare apples to apples. If you receive two separate contracts, make sure you counter them equally but *do not sign either one*. You need to be able to compare the merits of one versus the other without missing anything.

Even if you're only dealing with one buyer, you'll want to distil the contract into more simple and straightforward terms for your own reference and understanding. Use the *ListingDoor.com* worksheet, and again, *don't sign* until everything is agreed upon by all parties. If you sign the contract and then another offer comes back higher, you are obligated to go with the one you've signed.

The contract will state how much the buyer is putting down in earnest money and for a down payment. The more money down, the better and stronger the contract will be. The seller typically will pick the title company or escrow agent to hold the earnest money (usually 1 to 2 percent of the selling price), which goes toward the down payment or the closing costs.

You need to let the title company or escrow agent know that you're representing yourself. You'll need to obtain a title policy; the seller usually incurs this cost. The title policy acts as insurance for the buyer, letting them know you're delivering a clear title with no liens. No one wants a crazed aunt knocking on the door a year later, announcing that she's the home's real owner!

Some states use title companies, and others use escrow agents.

Home warranties are a safety net

Some buyers might bring up getting a home warranty at this point. Home warranties can be a good idea for both the buyer and the seller; they protect the buyer from having to pay for huge repairs on a home they haven't yet learned how to maintain, and they protect the seller from having to answer urgent phone calls from the buyer a month after the sale closes.

How do they work? First, you put down a fee—usually between $300 and $500, depending on the size of the home, which pays for a year's policy. The warranty covers a given set of systems and appliances in the home. If anything on the list breaks, the warranty company will call a provider to fix it. (Warranties tend to provide fixes rather than replacements—that's the downside.)

The new homeowner will be responsible for a small service fee, but the warranty company should pay for the repair.

If your buyer wants a home warranty, I'd suggest pricing one for your home and then crediting that amount to the buyer so that he or she can choose the warranty company. Warranties can make a slightly insecure buyer feel more secure and ready to sign a contract. For a few hundred dollars, the warranty can be an attractive selling point.

The home will be inspected after the earnest money contract is put into escrow, and then you and the buyer will have to negotiate the repairs.

Timing can be everything

In all my contracts, I add a "closing and funding plus forty–eight hours" stipulation to the possession date to give my sellers the guarantee that they'll have their money before they move their stuff out of the house.

Some buyers will agree to this and some won't. The ones who won't are the ones who are moving out of their houses in the morning and into yours in the afternoon. They don't want to spend the thousands of dollars it can cost to put a whole house worth of furniture in storage for a day to give the seller an extra forty–eight hours.

It's a subject worth broaching however because it gives you a little cushion of timing in case something goes awry at the last minute. I try to not let my clients move out until the house has funded. Sometimes it's possible, although sometimes it might not be.

In today's world, nothing is certain—especially finances. You don't want to deal with a problem like this. Ask for that forty–eight hours and if your buyer is amenable to giving it to you, by all means take it.

It's not over 'til the lender says it's approved

Your contract is contingent on the buyer getting financing unless you've been lucky enough to get a cash offer. Be prepared to help your buyer through the loan process, if necessary.

The process of getting a mortgage has changed since the recession. There are fewer applications, first of all. Some statistics put the current level of mortgage applications at 35 percent of what it was in 2007. Lenders are extremely cautious—in other words, you're now guilty till proven innocent rather than the other way around.

Your buyer needs a good credit score and be able to make a down payment to get the financing he or she needs to close on your home. You can do your part to avoid the hassle of having to start all over with another buyer by broaching this subject early in the process, preferably before you've done any serious negotiating.

Hopefully, you've already confirmed that your buyer is at least prequalified, if not preapproved, for a loan. Pre–qualifications are done by a simple calculation involving the buyer's assets and liabilities, but no information is confirmed. These days, you can get prequalified online in a minute or two.

Pre–approval, on the other hand, involves having a mortgage lender thoroughly check and verify all of the buyer's financial information, including the credit score. Neither is an absolute guarantee of a mortgage, and neither means the buyer is definitely going to be able to buy your home. But they're a good and necessary start for the process.

Before you and the buyer sign the contract, be certain that he or she is in communication with his or her lender of choice. Ask questions to make sure your buyer is on track with the deal in the same way you are.

Appraisal

Most agents do not even understand how the appraisal process has changed nor do they understand that when the Dodd–Frank Wall

Street Reform and Consumer Protection Act was passed it was only filled out 60% and every month more rules are added. Some agents are having problems getting homes to appraise, and if they had done a little work upfront, this would not be a problem.

Under the Dodd–Frank Act, most lenders have to go through an Appraisal Management Company that will assign an appraiser to a loan. Sometimes, the appraiser is familiar with your neighborhood and sometimes they are not. I suggest when the appraiser comes, handing him the comparable sales that you used to price your home (if you used *ListingDoor.com*, the sold homes on the IntelReport and a list of all the improvements or items that make your home special).

Appraisers want to do a good job and sometimes they don't notice updates you have done to the home. Provide them with a list of any updates or improvements. I have found that, even though, this is not the seller's responsibility, it helps with the appraisal.

Bottom Lines:

1. Know what the contract is and what it means.
2. Consider offering a home warranty.
3. Find out about your buyer's financial situation so you can get an idea of how likely the mortgage is to go through, but be prepared for last–minute glitches.
4. Ask for a "48–hour clause" to give yourself a little cushion of time at the very end.

"Companion Workbook" Download
http://po.st/workbook22

Chapter 10

SHERLOCK HOLMES IS LOOKING UNDER MY WATER HEATER WITH A FLASHLIGHT!

You're in the home stretch! That means it's time for the inspection report.

Does the idea of a professional going through your house looking for flaws make your skin crawl? Do you feel that the inspector is there to judge you on your home repair abilities, your housekeeping, and your asking price?

You've already had strangers looking through your house with a critical eye, deciding whether they wanted to buy. You might have had an appraiser walking around deciding what the house is worth. But now your house sale is almost complete, and you have to deal with the inspector! Who will he be and what will he find—and would it help to offer him a beer?

Everybody gets nervous about inspections. They can bring to mind the inspections you may have endured in gym class or the military. But remember, the inspector isn't trying to blame or label or judge you—just trying to find major flaws in the house that will need repair. Most inspections go just fine.

In a perfect world, you've taken good care of your home during your period of ownership, and you've done your necessary repair work before you even started showing it. But don't worry—if there's anything you need to take care of, the inspection report should tell you all this and (unfortunately) a little bit more.

FACT: *Inspection reports are not a wish-list for buyers.*

It can be common for buyers to misunderstand the purpose of an inspection. Buyers sometimes view inspection reports as a way to get a repair "wish list" that the seller then has to follow to the letter. But sellers are not required to have a perfect house, especially if the construction isn't new. Unless there's a health, structural, or safety component to the repairs, everything is negotiable. You're certainly *not* required to fix everything before you sell your home.

The real purpose of an inspection is simply to let the buyer know what they are buying before they commit their money or their bank's money. The process is similar to having a mechanic look over a used car before you buy it. When you do that, you don't go back to the used car dealership and demand that they fix everything before you buy the car. You might ask them to repair some obvious defect or flaw—but most likely, if you buy it, you'll understand that there will be some surface flaws you'll have to fix yourself if you want your vehicle to be perfect.

Getting ready for the inspection

It's important to know that the inspector is getting paid to find things wrong with your home, but at the same time, it's important to refrain from getting defensive against this process. Inspection is actually a form of protection for you just as much as it is for the buyer.

Your pre–inspection goal should be to set the stage for the

inspector. You want to make the impression quickly that you are a caring homeowner and that you've taken good care of your home.

If possible, you'll want to prepare all receipts, permits, and drawings for any maintenance and improvements you might have done over the years. This is not mandatory, but the inspector will find it helpful. You'll want to arrange things in your home so that the inspection will go easily. Here's a quick list of things to do:

1) Make sure all the light bulbs work in your home and that your air conditioner filters have been changed.
2) Create some kind of workspace around your furnaces and air conditioning units; your inspector is required to look at those, and he's going to need several feet of clearance to get in there with his equipment.
3) Your pilot lights should be lit.
4) The attic and garage should be relatively clear—basically, just move boxes away from the walls and equipment.
5) If there are keys for your electrical boxes, sprinkler systems, or the like, check that the keys are there.
6) Walk around the exterior of your house with the eyes of an inspector. Your gutters have to be clean, and your tree branches shouldn't be touching the windows or roof.
7) Tighten up your toilets if they're loose.
8) Caulk the joints around your windows.
9) All utilities need to be turned on.
10) Your inspector will run all appliances, so don't have clothes in your washer or dryer.
11) Remove anything that could block access to electrical panels or attics.

12) *Finally and most importantly*—just make sure that you're ahead of the game. Be certain that everything's working properly, and if something isn't, be ready to disclose this.

The NAHI.org site has another good, comprehensive list of what you need to do. If you've gone through all of these things, you should inform the inspector and the buyer: this will immediately remind both of them that you take pride in and respect the home that you're passing on.

If there was something you realized you should do but didn't have time to get to, disclose this openly. You'll get respect for being honest and saving the inspector time.

The inspector saw me in my pajamas!

Be ready and on time for the inspection. The house should be clean. If the inspection is at 9:00 a.m., chances are good that your inspector is going to get there a little early. They start by walking around the exterior of the home, so leave the shades down or curtains drawn unless you're dressed well in advance!

Offer the inspector something to drink. It can get very hot in those attic spaces, so a cold bottle of water is a big help. Let your inspector know who is in the home, and notify all occupants that you're awaiting an inspection. There's nothing worse than opening the door on a sleeping guest or college student!

Do not try to conceal any defects, since the buyer can sue you for damages if a problem arises. Do it right and don't try to hide anything. Disclose anything that might be considered structurally unusual about the house.

Most states require a seller's disclosure form to be given to buyers, and you want to be as thorough and straightforward as possible on this form. Disclosures are by no means deal breakers. Your buyer should understand that all homes have flaws. You, in turn, should remember that disclosure is the best insurance policy you could have.

The buyer typically pays for the inspection, so he or she will almost always be in attendance during the inspection process. Many buyers take this opportunity to let close friends and family come see the house.

It makes sense for you to at least meet the inspector and get a feel for how reasonable he will be. In this market, most of the extremely unreasonable inspectors are out of business. Show him anything that needs to be repaired before he begins the inspection. A realistic inspector leads to a realistic buyer.

Sellers aren't required to be there, and most inspectors don't want to be disturbed any more than they have to be. You don't have to babysit the inspector so I suggest coming and going as you would during a normal day while the inspection is in progress. By all means stay if you're uncomfortable having strangers in your home while you're away, just remember to stay out of the way.

This report makes my house sound so ... flawed

So, the inspection's done, and you've gotten your report. Don't ask to be there when the inspector is going over the report with the buyer—that's their business. You will be curious about what's on the report but wait until you get your own copy.

Most sellers ask for a copy of the inspection report to verify repairs—but there might be instances where you don't want one. Most states require you to disclose the inspection to any future buyers if this sale does not work out. In most states, you can refuse to receive the inspection report if the inspector seemed unreasonable or if the buyer cancels the contract without submitting a list of repairs.

Let's talk about what your responsibilities should and shouldn't be, so you can deal with these negotiations as professionally as possible. This is still an important part of making your way to a successful closing.

Some real estate agents have the tendency to drop the ball as soon as the money's in escrow, but negotiating your repairs can be as tricky as your first round of negotiations—so you have to keep going with consideration and common sense.

First, don't be alarmed by the inspection report, which might seem to turn small imperfections into major flaws. On paper, a tree branch touching the roof can become a fallen oak endangering the structure of your house. Inspectors are required to be overly cautious for liability reasons, so be prepared.

Keep in mind that the buyer is probably at the point where he wants things to work out if he has spent the money to have the home inspected. If you've had a structural, safety, or health issue (such as asbestos), come up with your house, know that you're probably never going to get a buyer who is okay leaving that as is and you'll need to get the repair done. If you're in the South, where the only two types of houses are those with termites and those about to get termites, be ready to take care of the critters if your house has an active infestation.

Your contract should have had a stipulation that any repairs above a certain amount would be negotiated (for details, see Chapter 9). Many factors are involved in your decision to make the repairs the buyer asks for or counter their repair wish list with one of your own.

Consider the market again before deciding. Are homes selling well in your area? Have you had to lower your asking price? Remember, if something bothered this buyer, chances are the next buyer will also want it fixed. However, there are buyers who use inspection reports to renegotiate the deal. It's in your best interest to do what the buyer asks if it is within reason.

FACT: *You have options when dealing with the inspection report.*

While it's good to prioritize the buyer's needs, you have the control here. You can refuse whatever you want, as long as you're ready to deal with the subsequent bargaining. Personally, I prefer to credit the buyer a set amount and let him or her make the repairs. You could add a line to the contract that goes something like this: "In lieu of any and all repairs, the buyer accepts the amount of X dollars. The property is being sold and purchased 'as is and where is,' in its present condition."

If you're having difficulty with the buyer, it might be prudent to remind him or her that the inspection report is intended to give an accurate picture of the home's condition—*not* to nit-pick it to pieces. If the inspector comes across as someone who thinks he's God's all-seeing eye on the real estate market, buyers can get confused into thinking that you're required to fix everything on the inspection report.

Hopefully, your buyer will realize that it's not ethical to renegotiate the purchase price because something minor comes to light in the inspection report. A cosmetic issue is never a necessary repair—but remember, if the repair poses a safety, structural, or physical *hazard*, chances are the next buyer is going to want it fixed.

Certain items are common on inspection reports. The inspector might state on his report that the roof needs to be replaced even if it's not leaking and still has a few good years left. This can be tough. You can either get a second opinion from a roof specialist or split the cost of the new roof. Keep in mind that some insurance companies will do a visual inspection of the roof before they will insure a home. If the roof is shot and leaking, chances are good that you'll have to replace it. If it's aging but not dead yet, the repair is negotiable, but it will probably keep the deal moving if you agree to split the repair costs.

The same thing can happen with an air conditioning system or hot water heater that has only a few years of life left. If these are fully functional, you're not required to repair or replace them—but if the buyers seem particularly concerned, negotiate and consider splitting the repair or replacement cost. As an alternative, you can purchase a home warranty to cover a possible future repair. For details, see Chapter 9.

Remember, your buyer might not ask for these repairs, even if they come up on the report—and that's why I suggest waiting to see the buyer's list of repairs before you act. I remember a seller who was extremely nervous about her kitchen appliances. The refrigerator was halfway through its expected lifespan and the stove had more than a few years on it. The seller was so worried that the prospective buyers would demand all new appliances.

As it turned out, the buyers could not have cared less. They had a state-of-the-art double stainless steel refrigerator and gourmet gas stove they were going to install before they moved in. In fact, one reason they selected that house was because it had room for their gigantic, special kitchen appliances. The seller worried for nothing.

If all this talk about repairs and negotiation is making you anxious—and you can't stand not knowing what the inspector might find—consider paying for an inspection yourself before listing your home. It will probably run $400–$600, and you'll be able to fix anything the inspector deems necessary at your own price and without the pressure of a buyer looking over your shoulder.

But there's a catch. In most states, you'll be legally obligated to disclose to potential buyers any problems found during this pre-inspection. If you decide to take this precautionary step, know that it will need to be addressed.

And, of course, it's always important to remember that you'd be going through all of these steps with or without a real estate agent. It's just part of the process.

You both have choices

Your buyer has four basic choices after an inspection report. The buyer can:

1. Ask you to make their requested repairs
2. Ask you to reduce the sales price in lieu of repairs
3. Request no repairs at all
4. Decline to buy the property

Those are really their only powers. They can't force you to make repairs, but they have the power to walk away from the sale if they can't live with your decisions on repairs.

As the seller, you have three choices. You can:

1. Agree to the buyer's request and make all the repairs.
2. Agree to part of the request and make some of the repairs, or create an allowance for repairs and stipulate in the contract that the house is being sold "as is."
3. Agree to make no repairs or credits at all.

If the negotiations are getting tricky, I suggest figuring out the amount you'd have to pay for the buyer's list of repairs and comparing that with the various costs involved in *not* selling your home. If you know, it will take a few more months to get to this point with another buyer, factor this into your response to the buyer's requests.

If negotiations extend past the option period for a few days, you can extend that period for the buyer's sake. Just get it in writing with both of your signatures and you'll have nothing to worry about.

FACT: *Repairs after inspection isn't an all-or-nothing process.*

One huge benefit of selling your home yourself is that you can negotiate personally and reasonably with the buyer. Middlemen *do not help* in this step any more than they do in negotiating a sales price. Real estate agents receive no training on how to deal with inspections and this is where deals fall apart. And just as in that process, middlemen can misinterpret, delay, or just generally get in the way.

Think about the number of steps each negotiation would take if you were working through agents. You would have to talk to your agent, then that agent would have to talk to the buyer's agent, then *that* agent would have to talk to the buyer—and the buyer's response would have to filter back through the same pipeline. Add the fact that both agents would be looking out for their own interests and have their own time constraints, and you can see that this process is never pretty or necessary.

If you cannot negotiate an agreement about repairs to both parties' satisfaction and you haven't included a home warranty in your contract discussions yet, you can still buy—or split the cost of—a home warranty for the buyer. That way, if whatever they're worried about does break in the near future, they'll be covered.

In reality, most buyers are reasonable. There are always a few who'd prefer to nickel and dime you, but you can avoid this by carefully evaluating your buyers and inspectors and setting the stage for an honest, straightforward transaction.

Bottom Lines:

1. Inspections aren't bad or scary if you prepare in advance.
2. Be polite and cooperative during the inspection.
3. Requests are just requests, not ultimatums.
4. Be flexible, and if you tire of the negotiation process, consider offering a repair allowance or home warranty that covers all repairs.

"Companion Workbook" Download
http://po.st/workbook22

Chapter 11

HEY, I JUST SOLD MY HOUSE!

You've found a buyer, agreed on a price and other details, and your house is as good as sold—and you've done this without the help of a real estate agent! You should be feeling confident now. If your confidence level is high, you can take this deal all the way to the finish line, all by yourself.

You can find a great deal of free help on the Internet these days but you might feel more secure if you have someone with legal experience look over the paperwork and answer your questions.

Don't hesitate to hire a real estate attorney if you want someone to help you through this stage. A few hours of an attorney's time won't cost much and will reassure you that you've taken care of all the necessary details. Even real estate agents will sometimes want you to hire an attorney if there is a boundary or title issue. In that case, you still have to pay the attorney.

Choose a licensed attorney who has knowledge and experience handling real estate transactions. If you like, the attorney can see you through the rest of the process—until the very last paper has been signed. The attorney's fee will be much less than a real estate agent's commission would have been.

Real estate contracts are fill–in–the–blank and largely self–explanatory, but it won't hurt to have an expert look them over. Some people do their taxes with TurboTax and then have their CPA look over the paperwork and give it their blessing.

Whether you hire an attorney or do these final steps by yourself, you're going to want to know what's going on.

Like so much of the information in this book, the advice I give you here is prevention–minded and meant to keep you from encountering any problems that might shut down your deal at this crucial moment.

The opening act of the big closing

Your buyer should already have applied for the mortgage by the time you sign the earnest money contract. At this point, the buyer's mortgage is in the hands of the lender for processing. During processing, there's usually an appraisal from a lender–approved group of appraisers; specific policies vary from company to company.

I suggest giving the lender's appraiser a copy of whatever research you did in your price analysis. If you paid for a professional appraisal, you might want to hand that over if it is close to the sales price. Appraisers are now picked out of a pool at the lender's discretion making it very likely you'll be more familiar with your area than the appraiser is.

After the appraisal, the application moves to the underwriter, who reviews and approves the mortgage. The file is then sent to the lending company's attorneys for review; they check the application, the title commitment, and the survey.

The closer verifies all fees and terms and gives the title company instructions for how the closing settlement statement (also referred to as a HUD statement) will work to reflect the particular circumstances of the sale.

What do I need to watch out for?

Two common problems arise at this stage: the borrower not having homeowner's insurance and the surveyor not completing a survey.

These steps should have been taken care of during processing, and it's the buyer's responsibility to see that they are.

The buyer should have put in an application for homeowner's insurance starting at least a week if not longer before closing because if the buyer doesn't have insurance, the lender won't disburse any money. You might want to give your buyer a friendly reminder to be sure this has been taken care of.

The lender should also have sent a surveyor to survey your home. If you have a survey that's five years old or less and you haven't made any additions or major changes to your home, offer it to the buyer. Some lenders/title companies will accept the survey, which could save the buyer up to $1,000.

During this window, the title company or escrow agent will contact you if you have a mortgage on the property. They'll request the name of your lender so they can get the exact payoff amount on your loan.

Prior to closing (usually the day before), it's customary to walk through the house with your buyer as a courtesy. Most states give them the right to this final visual inspection before they sign. Your house should be spotless at this point (more about this in the next section), but you should clear out any leaves or trash remaining on the property. Or, if they agree, you can offer to credit the buyer an amount of money to have it taken care of.

Utilities are another loose end to take care of at this time. The buyer needs to transfer the utilities to his or her name at least a week before moving in. Since some utility companies will not transfer the service until the seller has notified them that he wants to have the utilities in his name disconnected, you can take the initiative on this so your buyer doesn't end up without power for the first few days after moving in. What a buzz kill!

You should get a copy of the exact closing costs and settlement statement before the closing itself, but sometimes the lending company is scrambling for documents and can't get it to you until an hour before. This is normal. Review the closing statement when you get it.

Closing will take place at either a title company or escrow agent's office, depending on your state. You'll meet with the buyer and sign all the documents. You should both bring legal forms of identification.

You will need to supply information about where you want the proceeds from the sale sent.

After you've signed, the title company will send the papers to the lender, the lender will authorize the funding to be released, and *it will finally all be over!*

Give the new homeowners the keys! When the deal has finally closed and is fully funded, you can go ahead and cancel your homeowner's insurance.

Who pays for what, again?

This can all get a little confusing, and just for a review, here's a list of who should be taking care of what. This is the way the responsibilities are customarily divided, although it's not written in stone.

The seller's responsibility:

1) The title policy, issued by the title company
2) Property taxes up until the closing date (this will be on the closing statement)

The buyer's responsibility:

1) The inspection
2) The appraisal
3) The loan fees—although some buyers will ask the seller to

pay a "point" of their loan

4) Insurance

5) Property taxes from the closing date forward

Staying classy

Zappos, the online shoe retailer, is famous for its exemplary business practices. The company lives by its CEO's guiding principle:

> *"People may not remember exactly what you did, but they will always remember how you made them feel."*

Why do I quote this? In your transition period, you need to remember this idea. You might be dog–tired from the process of moving out, but you can't cut corners. Make sure you allow for time to clean the house you just sold before the buyer takes possession. If you are too worried, tired, or stressed to deal with cleaning, hire a cleaning service. If you cannot afford one, ask a few friends to pitch in and help or chip in and pay for one.

You always want to turn the house over in a condition that approaches spotless, with clean interiors, a mowed yard, and a clean pool (if you have one).

I'd even suggest going the extra mile by buying some toilet paper, paper towels, hand soap, and bottled water to leave on the kitchen counter for your buyers. If you want to go *another* extra mile, leave a bottle of wine for the new homeowners so they can celebrate in style.

I suggest you take care of these tasks before you start trying to move so they don't stress you out while you're exhausted from putting all your things in boxes. Keep your parting gifts in a little shopping bag so you don't lose them, or pack them by accident, and set them out as the last thing you do before you leave.

FACT: *Being gracious goes a long way.*

This advice isn't just a matter of etiquette—it's a matter of practicality. After all, you've done a lot of work and when you're out, you want to be out. You want to feel good about what you've done and, more importantly, avoid any complications or problems. The last thing you want is to pick up the phone a week later and hear, "Well, we have a little problem."

The buyer might feel slighted or even cheated if you leave your home in a careless condition—and trust me, when the buyer starts to feel cheated is when the problems begin. If you've done everything right up to this point, nothing ties up loose ends like cleaning the house and leaving a few conveniences. I have never had a problem with a transaction, and I am convinced that this final touch is one of the biggest reasons why.

In the book Blink [http://po.st/simplesold32]. Malcolm Gladwell lays out a convincing argument to support this idea. He says that our judgments are not based on carefully considered reasoning but on what he calls "thin-slicing," which is a quick, spontaneous, subconscious moment of decision and perception that guides the rest of our actions. The split-second when the new buyer walks into their home will determine how they react to this completed transaction. Call it taking care of the customer or call it the power of impressions—either way, I can't overstate the importance of giving the buyer a really great first split-second.

Also, as the seller it is 100% your responsibility to get the keys to the buyer. Don't ask them to come pick them up; they've just spent a lot of money, so do them the small courtesy of bringing them the keys. You should have two to four keys to give them as well as all the garage door openers and any user manuals you have for the appliances. If you have a list of service people who have been servicing your home, give the new owners that list as well.

Incidentally, this is another case where your common sense and graciousness give you an advantage over the rest of the industry. I once met for coffee with a real estate agent who wouldn't stop complaining because the home she had just sold was left dirty and "it was not her responsibility to have it clean." She told me with exasperation that the other agent should have written it into the contract.

As she spoke, it was all I could do to keep from blurting, "What are you thinking? This is your *reputation* on the line." I would have had a cleaning service over there in a second and paid for it out of pocket if I had to. This is just a good business practice that follows the theories of Tony Hsieh and Malcolm Gladwell.

The buyer might not have understood exactly how much work or expense went into cleaning the house, but they'll always remember that first split–second when they walked into a spotless house and felt so happy to finally be home.

Bottom Lines:

1. If this sounds like a lot of work, remember this: You Unless your state requires that you get an attorney, you can handle the paperwork yourself. Consult an attorney if it makes you feel better.
2. Give your buyer a wonderful first split–second in their new home.
3. Bow out gracefully and leave toilet paper.

"Companion Workbook" Download
http://po.st/workbook22

Chapter 12

THAT WASN'T SO HARD! WHY DOESN'T EVERYBODY DO THIS?

Well, it's over. If this is the first time you've sold a house on your own, all I can say is—congratulations! You saved yourself thousands of dollars and learned something that many Americans are learning. Now you know you really can sell your home yourself.

Having done it once, you can do it again. Although we like to think that our current home is "the one," it's important to remember that the average person moves twelve times in his or her life. In four or five more years, you might be selling another home.

Hold onto this book! Technology will change, but that will only make it easier for homeowners to sell their own homes. There's no reason that you should go back to using a real estate agent now that you know how to do a real estate agent's job!

Hopefully, you've found yourself a great new home to move into—and if you used your common sense, you didn't need an agent on that end, either. Buying a home without an agent will involve many of the same steps that you've just read about, learned, and put into action (or steps you are currently gearing up to take, after your first read!).

Be the buyer that you wish *your* buyer had been. Do your research on the market you're looking to buy into. Figure out how much equity you'll have after the home sale (and do a little happy dance because of how much bigger your equity is than it would have been had you used an agent).

Search for homes within your price point and visit open houses. When you see the home, remember that you can negotiate the exclusions, and take into account recent remodels or renovations.

Make an offer that reflects the research you've done about that home—using those old three "C's"—and be ready to negotiate like a professional. Start the mortgage process, watch the home get inspected, and then close the deal. It's that simple.

You can play a part in helping revolutionize the real estate industry into finally becoming consumer oriented. You can tell the world that you sold your home yourself! Share your experience with your friends. Real estate is a natural hot topic for conversation because, well, you just can't get away from it! Everyone lives somewhere. Eventually, everyone's going to move somewhere else.

Your story is relevant to any person with the common sense to see that there's no reason to give a real estate agent a huge commission anymore.

The real estate industry will adjust if more American consumers take matters into their own hands.

When you encounter friends who are thinking of selling, point them to the path you went down. Be honest about the problems and frustrations, because the biggest reward (6 percent of your home's value in your pocket) speaks for itself. And there's nothing like the feeling of satisfaction you get from doing it yourself and doing it well.

So again, congratulations. Spread the word! We're revolutionizing real estate, one house at a time.

Bottom Lines:

1. Be proud of yourself. You've done something not many people have tried, and it worked out well!
2. Tell people about your experience of selling your own home, to give them courage.
3. Hang onto this book for the next time you sell—or give it to someone who needs the information now.

"Companion Workbook" Download
http://po.st/workbook22

SOURCES

Levin, Rich. "Top 10 Negotiating Rules for Realtors". www.theredx.com/blog/2010/07/newsletter-july-2010-top-10-negotiating-rules-for-realtors

Gantenbein, Douglas. "Realty Bites: Why do you still need an agent to buy a home?" *Slate*, August 16, 2004. www.slate.com/articles/life/a_fine_whine/2004/08/realty_bites.html

Justice, Glen. "Lobbying to Sell Your House." *The New York Times*, January 12, 2006. www.nytimes.com/2006/01/12/business/12realtors.html

Taylor, Candace. "Residential Real Estate Firms and Brokers Need to Think Thin." http://therealdeal.com/blog/2009/05/08/residential-real-estate-firms-and-brokers-need-to-think-thin/

Streitfeld, David. "Housing Market Slows as Buyers Get Picky." *The New York Times*, June 16, 2010. www.nytimes.com/2010/06/17/business/economy/17slump.html

Fletcher, June. "What Stays and What Goes When You Sell?" *The Wall Street Journal,* March 4, 2011. http://www.wsj.com/articles/SB10001424052748703580004576180602861220040

Nicholle–Nelson, Tara. "6 Things That Turn Home Buyers Off (and What Sellers Can Do To Prevent It)!" *Business Insider,* February 23, 2011. www.businessinsider.com/6–things–that–turn–home–buyers–off–and–what–sellers–can–do–to–prevent–it–2012–9

Alberico, Donna. "To Sell an Apartment, Brokers Suggest Spending on the Details." *The New York Times,* February 21, 2011. www.constructionrepair.net/geraldine–onorato–represented–a–client–selling–a.html

Zavala, Melissa. "68% of Buyers are not Satisfied with Their Agents." *Realuso,* January 14, 2015. http://realuoso.com/editorials/68–buyers–not–satisfied–agent/

FAQS

Will a property I sell myself be at a competitive disadvantage compared to properties sold by real estate agents?

No—and in a lot of ways, you'll have an advantage. First of all, today's buyers find their homes on the Internet on their own time. If they like your home, they're going to contact you no matter what—and the odds are good that they'll be happier dealing with you than with an agent. It is no secret that a huge number of homes are languishing on the market and expire before the agent ever gets the home sold. Do a Google search and you'll see the amount of training material the real estate industry offers to teach their agents how to persuade sellers to renew their listings for a year. There is no magic in what a real estate agent does.

To give you an example of the advantages of selling your home yourself, think about signs. When you list with an agent, they get to place a mini-billboard in your yard that includes a tiny bit of advertising for your home and a huge amount of advertising for their company. The whole industry should have moved on to customized signs a long time ago—but they haven't. You'll have a significant advantage by tailoring your on-the-ground marketing plan to your home, including your FOR SALE sign.

Do homes sell for more when listed with a real estate agent?

That's what the National Association of REALTORS—funded

by real estate agents—says, but there's no independent data to support their statistics. If a real estate agent tells you they can get you more money for your home, ask them to bring you a buyer; if they can't, they need to leave you alone to sell your house. Far too many listings handled by agents expire unsold.

An agent's opinion is not going to get your home sold. It's easy for people to make guesses and conjectures, but to win in today's market you have to deal with hard facts.

How much time and effort is this really going to take?

It takes about as much time to sell your house as it takes to plan a long vacation. The marketing side requires the most time up front, but once you've gathered your facts, it shouldn't take you more than a few hours to get your marketing plan started. You'd have to gather that same information for an agent if you used one. And the process has been streamlined for you on *Simple and SOLD.*

If you're still not convinced, take the amount you'd pay in commission to a real estate agent and divide it by the number of hours it takes to plan a vacation. The result should help you see that time you put into selling your house will be time well spent.

A real estate agent told me it would be dangerous to sell my own home, since I'd be letting strangers in my house all the time. Should I be worried?

Unfortunately, you have to let strangers in your home to sell it. But this is a moot point since you have to do it with or without a real estate agent. Remember that you can open your home any way you want: you can take down information for safety purposes, or you can schedule your viewing appointments so you won't be alone in the house. You also have the right to stop the process if you become uncomfortable with anyone. It is something real estate agents face, too.

Do I need to use the MLS to get the exposure I need for my home?

First, understand what the MLS is. It is not a marketing venue for homes, it's a way for brokers to negotiate compensation with each other, so Real Estate Agent A can tell Real Estate Agent B, "sell my listing and I will pay you X." Period.

Look at Zillow, Trulia, and Yahoo! Real Estate and you'll see how much the MLS has been eclipsed. It's become just an outdated method for real estate agents to protect their turf. Some systems are not even Mac compatible.

What is the NAR?

NAR is the acronym for the National Association of REALTORS®, ranked #2 (2012–2015/Q1) by OpenSecrets.org's list of the top Washington lobbying spenders. It's the organization about which Joe Nocera of the *New York Times* once wrote: "You have to wonder sometimes what they're smoking over there at the National Association of REALTORS."

The NAR has stayed under the radar while doing a monstrous amount of damage to the economy, the housing market, and most importantly, the consumer. Bloodhound Realty blog states (this blog does a great job of exposing the NAR), "It was the NAR that lobbied for each law and rule change that resulted in the housing boom, the subprime lending catastrophe, the wanton bundling of fraudulent loans, the on–going subsidization of the secondary mortgage market, etc. The villain behind all the villains in the collapse of the American economy is the National Association of REALTORS."

"The real estate licensing laws, written in their original form *by* the NAR, exist to limit competition in real estate brokerage, eliminating alternative sources of real estate brokerage to artificially sustain higher commissions for NAR brokers."

Don't most people trust real estate agents to get them the best deal?

Unfortunately, many people don't trust them at all. In one public opinion poll, they ranked lower than used car salesmen in terms of ethics.

In all fairness, it's not the behavior of real estate agents that has been unethical; it's the way their organization, the NAR, has worked to ruthlessly block their competition. As I see it, and as most Americans see it, competition is for the competent. You own your home, so you should have the choice to sell it any way you choose.

The NAR got a huge public slap on the wrist in 2008 from the Justice Department when the organization tried to stop real estate agents without physical offices from participating in the MLS. The Justice Department sued the NAR to allow mobile, Internet–based brokers—the kind who operate from laptops and Starbucks instead of fancy offices—to practice their trade.

I think the NAR should be ashamed of making taxpayers pay for this lawsuit, which (in the words of the DOJ itself) "requires NAR to allow Internet–based residential real estate brokers to compete with traditional brokers." The Department said the settlement would enhance competition in the real estate brokerage industry, giving consumers more choices, better service, and lower commission rates. NAR is now bound by a ten–year settlement to ensure that it abides by the agreement.

But don't real estate agents operate under a Code of Ethics?

In my opinion, anyone who needs an organization to tell them how to be ethical probably doesn't understand the code of ethics that they're swearing to uphold.

GLOSSARY

You will never need most of these terms, but here are everyday translations in case they do come up:

Adjustable-rate mortgage (ARM)

A mortgage in which the interest rate changes periodically, based on an index that reflects the current credit market. Some ARMs allow the lender to change the interest rate at their discretion, according to the terms of the mortgage agreement.

Amenities

Features that enhance the value of property such as big closets, new appliances, or a pool.

Amortization

The process by which your loan principal decreases over time. A portion of each mortgage payment goes toward interest and the rest goes toward reducing the loan amount.

Amortization schedule / Amortization table

A table that shows how much of each payment will be applied to the principal and how much to interest, over the life of your loan, and when you can expect the balance to hit zero.

Application / Loan application

The form used to apply for a mortgage. The borrower supplies information about income, savings, assets, debts, and other financial details, and the lender verifies the information's accuracy.

Appraisal

A written report of the current market value of a piece of real estate that reflects the location, physical condition, market conditions, and recent sales of comparable properties. Lenders order a current appraisal before making a loan.

Appraised value

The appraiser's opinion of the value of your home.

Appraiser

A licensed professional who calculates the value of your home. The lender chooses the appraiser.

Assessed value / Assessment

The dollar value placed on property by a public tax assessor for the purpose of taxation.

Attrition/Absorption rate

The number of homes per month sold in a specified price range in a specified area.

Chain of title

A written record of who has owned the property in the past.

Clear title

A title free of liens or legal questions as to ownership of the property.

Closing

The final step in a real estate transaction, when the buyer and seller come together and execute all necessary documents to transfer the property from the seller to the buyer. The deal is considered "closed" either when all documents have been signed and the money has changed hands (when the deal has been "funded") or when all documents have been recorded at the courthouse—depending on the state.

Closing costs

Costs associated with transfer of property, which are specified on your closing statement. The title company/escrow agent can give you an estimate of what these costs will be.

Closing statement

Also called a "HUD–1 Statement" or "Settlement Statement," this form details all cost/fees for the seller and buyer in a real estate transaction.

Cloud on title / Defect on title

Any condition that adversely affects the transfer of real estate, such as a lien on property or unpaid property taxes. These conditions are revealed by a title search and need to be removed—usually by deed, release, or court action—before the closing.

Co-borrower

An additional individual who is obligated on the loan and title of the property.

Collateral

The property on which a loan (mortgage) is made. If the borrower does not pay according to the terms of the loan, the lender may seize the collateral, which is called "foreclosure."

Common area assessments

Fees paid to a homeowners association by the owners of individual housing units to be used to maintain the property's common areas. Sometimes called "homeowners association fees" (in a planned unit development) or "condo fees" in a condominium or co–operative apartment.

Common areas

The areas of a planned unit development (PUD) or condominium that are used by all housing unit owners, including recreational facilities, hallways, and parking areas. Housing unit owners share the expense of maintaining common areas.

Community property

Property that is owned jointly by both spouses.

Comparable sales / Comps

Recent sales of similar properties in the same area, used to help determine a property's market value.

Competition

The number of homes in a specific area that are for sale in a similar price range.

Condominium / Condo

A form of property ownership where specified portions of a property (usually single housing units) are individually owned, and the owners have legal rights to use—and financial obligations to maintain—the common areas.

Condominium conversion

The process of changing the ownership of an existing building (usually a rental project) into individually owned units.

Contingency

A condition that must be met before a contract is legally binding.

Earnest money contract / Purchase contract

A written agreement between seller and buyer setting the terms for the purchase of the property.

Carrying cost / Holding cost

The cost of owning a property, including mortgage payments, taxes, insurance, maintenance, and other expenses.

Conventional mortgage

A loan not guaranteed by a government agency such as the Federal Housing Administration (HUD) or U.S. Department of Veteran Affairs. Conventional mortgages usually have fixed rates and terms.

Creditor

A person to whom money is owed.

Credit report / Credit history

A detailed report of an individual's credit history, prepared by a credit bureau and used by a lender in determining an applicant's credit–worthiness.

Days on the market / DOM

How many days a property has been on the market.

Debt

An amount owed to another.

Deed

The legal document conveying title to a property.

Deed in lieu of foreclosure

A process in which a borrower in default on a mortgage gives the property's title to the lender, through mutual agreement. The deed in lieu is usually meant to delay or avoid foreclosure and may have advantages to both lender and borrower, although it may not improve the borrower's credit record.

Deed of trust

The legal title to property that is transferred to a trustee. Some states, like California, record deeds of trust instead of mortgages.

Default

Failure to make a mortgage payment within a specified period of time. In most cases, a loan is considered to be in default if a payment has not been made within thirty days of the due date.

Delinquent

The condition of a loan for which the borrower has failed to make mortgage payments when they are due. A loan may be considered delinquent on the first day a payment is missed unless the mortgage contract specifies a grace period. When a loan payment is more than thirty days late, most lenders consider the loan delinquent and report the late payment to credit bureaus.

Discount point

One percent of the loan amount, paid in addition to the 1 percent loan origination fee, which can be used to lower the interest rate on the loan's balance. Discount points are usually used only in FHA and VA loans.

Down payment

The amount of money a property buyer pays in cash at the beginning of the transaction, which is not financed with the mortgage.

Earnest money

The cash deposit a potential homebuyer makes to show serious intent to purchase a property. The earnest money is held in escrow until the transaction is complete.

Easement

A right–of–way that allows people other than the property owner to access the property.

Eminent domain

The right of a government to take private property for public use upon payment of the property's fair market value.

Encroachment

An improvement such as a building, fence, or driveway that is found to have been built on another person's property. An encroachment is usually the fault of incorrect surveys or builder miscalculations.

Encumbrance

Anything that affects or limits the title to a property, including mortgages, leases, easements, or restrictions.

Equity

A homeowner's financial interest in the property. Equity is the difference between the home's fair market value and the balance still owed for the mortgage and other liens on the home.

Escrow

Money held by a third party (usually a title company or escrow agent) to be released upon fulfillment of a condition. Earnest money in a real estate transaction is put into escrow and delivered to the seller when the transaction is closed.

Escrow account

An account set up by a lender to hold separate funds for the purpose of paying insurance and taxes on a property. The lender collects this money as part of the mortgage payment, puts it into an escrow account, and then pays the insurance and property taxes for the homeowner.

Examination of title

A report on a property's title with information drawn from public records or an abstract of the title.

Excellent condition

A description of property that is in move–in or mint condition.

Exclusions

Personal property attached to the home, such as appliances or fixtures, which will not be included when the property is sold.

Façade

The exterior of a property.

Fair market value

The price a non–desperate buyer is willing to pay to a non–desperate seller for a property.

Federal Housing Administration (FHA)

An agency of the U.S. Department of Housing and Urban Development (HUD) whose main purpose is to insure residential mortgage loans made by private lenders. The FHA sets standards for construction and underwriting but does not lend money or plan or construct housing.

Fee simple

Absolute ownership of a property and entitlement to all rights to the property.

FHA mortgage

A mortgage insured by the Federal Housing Administration (FHA), sometimes called a "government loan." A VA loan is also a government loan.

Financing

Borrowing money to purchase property.

Fixed-rate mortgage

A mortgage in which the interest rate does not change (is fixed) during the entire term of the loan.

Fixture

Personal property that is attached in a permanent manner to real estate and which will stay with the house when it is sold, such as built–in bookcases and appliances.

Flood insurance

Insurance that covers property loss from flooding.

Foreclosure

An order of the courts through which a lender reclaims a property after a borrower has failed to make timely mortgage payments. The property may be sold at public auction and the proceeds applied to the mortgage debt.

FSBO

For Sale By Owner.

Full bath

A bathroom with a bath or shower.

Funding

When the buyer receives the funds from the sale of property.

Grantee

The person to whom an interest in real property is conveyed; the buyer of the property.

Grantor

The person conveying an interest in real property; the seller of the property.

Half bath

A bathroom without a bathtub or a shower.

Interest rate

The cost of borrowing money from a lender.

Jack and Jill bath

A bathroom with two doors, usually accessible from two bedrooms.

Judgment

A legal document that requires the repayment of a debt. The courts may place a lien against a debtor's real property as collateral for the judgment's creditor.

Jumbo loan / Non-conforming loan

A loan that exceeds loan limits set by the government–sponsored mortgage programs Fannie Mae and Freddie Mac. The 2011 loan limit is $417,000 for most states.

Lease

A written agreement between the property owner and a tenant specifying the payment and conditions under which the tenant may possess (rent) real estate for a specified period of time.

Legal description

A property description that is recognized by law as sufficient to locate and identify the property.

Lender

The institution making the loan or the individual representing the firm making the loan.

Liabilities

A person's financial obligations. Anything you owe money on, whether it is a long–term or short–term debt.

Liability insurance

Insurance coverage that offers protection against claims alleging that a property owner's negligence or inappropriate action resulted in bodily injury or property damage to another party. Liability insurance is usually part of a homeowner's insurance policy.

Lien

A legal claim against a property for money owed. A mortgage is considered a lien.

Loan

A sum of borrowed money (principal) that is repaid, generally with interest.

Loan application

The form used to apply for a mortgage. The borrower supplies information about income, savings, assets, debts and other financial details, and the lender verifies the information's accuracy.

Loan officer

An individual who serves as an intermediary between the lending institutions and the borrower. Loan officers help the borrower obtain a mortgage and oversee the lending process.

Loan origination

A term used by lenders to refer to the process of obtaining a new loan.

Loan servicing

Collecting payments due on a loan. Some lenders service their own loans, and others use servicing companies to process payments, send statements, manage the escrow/impound account, provide collection efforts on delinquent loans, ensure that insurance and property payments are made on the property, handle pay–offs and assumptions, and provide a variety of other services.

Loan-to-value ratio (LTV)

The percentage relationship between the amount of the loan and the appraised value of the property. The higher the LTV, the riskier the loan is to the lender.

Lock-in

A specific interest rate that the lender guarantees for a specific amount of time at a certain cost.

Lock-in period

The time period during which the lender has guaranteed an interest rate to a borrower.

Loft

Open living space that contains high ceilings, large windows, and open space.

Lot

A measured section of land.

Merged credit report

A credit report that includes data from two or more of the major credit reporting bureaus.

Modification

A change in the terms of a mortgage, made by the lender, without requiring the borrower to refinance.

Mortgage

A legal document that pledges property to the lender as security for payment of a debt. Instead of mortgages, some states use "first trust deeds."

Mortgage broker

A mortgage company or person who originates loans and then places those loans with a variety of other lending institutions; an intermediary between the lenders and the borrower who helps to expedite the process.

Mortgagee

The lender.

Mortgage insurance (MI)

Insurance that covers the lender against default on a home loan. Often mistakenly referred to as PMI (private mortgage insurance), which is actually the name of one of the larger mortgage insurers. Mortgage insurance is required for most loans in which the borrower's down payment is less than 20 percent. FHA loans and certain first–time homebuyer programs require mortgage insurance regardless of the LTV ratio.

Mortgagor

The borrower.

Negative amortization / Neg Am

The amount of a loan payment that is less than the actual interest cost on a property. The negative amount is added to the note, increasing the loan amount. The borrower is deferring part of the interest payment.

Note / Promissory note

A legal document that obligates a borrower to repay a mortgage loan at a stated interest rate during a specified period of time.

Note rate / Interest rate

The interest rate stated on a mortgage note.

No-points loan / Zero-points loan

A loan for which no "points" were prepaid to reduce the interest rate. Almost all lenders offer loans at "no points." Pre–paying an interest point can reduce the interest rate by ¼ to ½ percent.

Offer

An expression of desire to purchase a property at a specific price. The first step that leads to the purchase of property.

Offer accepted

When the owner of the property agrees and accepts the terms of the buyer's contract.

Open house

A specific time when a property is open for inspection by prospective buyers. Most open houses are held on Sunday afternoons.

Original principal balance

The total amount of a mortgage before any payments are made.

Origination fee

A fee charged by the lender for creating a loan. Origination fees are typically one percent of the loan amount.

Owner financing

When the property seller provides all or part of the financing.

Personal property

Any property that is not real property. In a real estate transaction, the furnishings are the things the seller takes along when he moves.

PITI

The sum of a monthly mortgage payment, which includes the required portion of the loan principal and interest plus required property taxes, homeowners insurance, and mortgage insurance.

PITI reserves

The money a lender requires a borrower to have in reserve in order to qualify for a loan, usually equal to two to three months' worth of payments on the loan principal and interest plus required property taxes, homeowners insurance, and mortgage insurance.

Point

One percent of the amount of a mortgage.

Pre-approval

A loosely used term that means a borrower has filled a loan application and provided debt, income, and savings information but no underwriter has reviewed the information and deemed the borrower credit–worthy. Pre–approvals are based on an assumed loan amount and interest rate and estimated property taxes, insurance, and other expenses. Pre–approvals are loaded with fine print and are not absolute guarantees of a mortgage.

Prepayment

Any amount paid to reduce the principal balance of a loan before the due date.

Prepayment penalty

A fee that may be charged to a borrower who pays off a loan before it is due.

Pre-qualification

A loan officer's written opinion of the ability of a borrower to qualify for a home loan. Before pre–qualifying a loan applicant, the loan officer makes inquiries (usually verbal) about debt, income, and savings and may or may not review the applicant's credit report. Pre–qualification is less useful than pre–approval.

Prime rate

The interest rates that banks charge to their preferred customers. Changes in the prime rate are widely publicized in the news media.

Principal

The amount borrowed or, as you make payments, the amount remaining unpaid. Paying off your principal reduces the balance of your mortgage.

Principal balance

The outstanding balance on a mortgage.

Promissory note

A written promise to repay a specified amount over a specified period of time.

Property tax

Taxes on a specific property issued by state or local authorities.

Planned Unit Development (PUD)

A project or subdivision that includes common property that is owned and maintained by a homeowners' association for the benefit and use of the individual PUD unit owners.

Purchase agreement / Earnest money contract

A written contract signed by the buyer and seller stating the terms and conditions under which a property will be sold.

Qualifying ratios

Calculations used in determining whether a borrower can qualify for a mortgage.

Quitclaim deed

A deed in which the grantor transfers property (with no warranty regarding the status of the property) to a grantee, used most often in transactions between family members or business entities, or in other exceptional circumstances.

Rate lock

A commitment issued by a lender to a borrower guaranteeing a specified interest rate for a specified period of time.

Real property

All land, buildings, improvements, trees, minerals, and mineral rights on a piece of property, as well as anything firmly attached to the property.

Recorder / County Clerk / Registrar of Deeds

The public official who keeps records of transactions that affect real property.

Recording

A system that records the title of real estate and the details of a properly executed legal document, such as a deed, a mortgage note, a satisfaction of mortgage, or an extension of mortgage. Recording is usually done in a government office and makes the document a part of the public record.

Remaining balance / Principal balance

The amount of a loan that has not yet been repaid.

Right of first refusal

A provision in a contract that requires the owner of a property to give another party the first opportunity to purchase or lease the property before he or she offers it for sale or lease to others.

Right of ingress or egress

The right to enter or leave an area.

Right of survivorship

When two or more people own a piece of property and one dies, the right of survivors to acquire the interest of the deceased.

Sale-leaseback

An arrangement in which a seller closes on a property and deeds the property to the buyer, and then the buyer leases the property back to the seller.

Sale price / Purchase price

The amount of money for which a property sells.

Second mortgage

Money borrowed against a piece of property in addition to the first mortgage, usually in the form of a home equity loan, that is "subordinate" to the first mortgage—meaning that if the borrower defaults on a loan, the first mortgage will be paid off before the second mortgage.

Secondary market

The financial market for mortgages that are bundled together and sold to investors.

Secured loan

A loan backed by collateral. In a home sale, the collateral of a secured loan is the real estate.

Security

The property that will be pledged as collateral for a loan.

Settlement statement

See Closing Statement.

Single family residence

A freestanding residential home.

Subdivision

A housing development that is created by dividing a tract of land into individual lots for sale or lease.

Survey

A drawing or map showing the precise legal boundaries of a property as well as the location of improvements, easements, rights of way, encroachments, and other physical features.

Tenancy in common

A type of property ownership in which two or more people jointly possess a property, but if one dies, the ownership does not automatically pass to the surviving owner or owners, as it would in "joint tenancy."

Term

A specified period of time.

Third-party originator / Mortgage broker

A person or company that prepares loan applications from borrowers and submits the applications to lenders.

Title

A legal document showing a person's right to, or ownership of, a property.

Title commitment

An offer to issue a title insurance policy. The title commitment describes the various conditions, exclusions, and exceptions that will apply to the policy and is typically issued by the title company or escrow agent.

Title company

A company that specializes in examining and insuring titles to real estate.

Title insurance

Insurance that protects the lender and the buyer against loss from title defects such as liens against the property. The state's insurance department typically sets title insurance rates.

Title search

A check of the title records to ensure that the seller is the legal owner of the property and that there are no liens or outstanding claims against the property. A title search is done by either the title company or escrow agent, depending on your state.

Title policy / Title commitment

A guarantee that the title company has searched the records for that property and that the title is clear of any liens, judgments, or fraud.

Transfer tax

State or local tax payable when a title passes from one owner to another.

Truth-in-lending

A federal law that requires lenders to disclose fully, in writing, the terms and conditions of a mortgage, including the annual percentage rate (APR) and other charges.

Two- to four-family property

A property that consists of a structure that provides living space (dwelling units) for more than one family, although ownership of the structure is by a single deed. If the property includes living space for two families, it is sometimes called a "duplex," or for four families, a "fourplex."

Trustee

A fiduciary that holds or controls property for the benefit of another.

Utilities

Services such as electricity, gas, and water.

VA mortgage

A mortgage that is guaranteed by the U.S. Department of Veterans Affairs (VA).

Walk-through inspection

An additional inspection of the property by the buyer just before closing meant to ensure that the property does not have any new damage.

Made in United States
North Haven, CT
21 September 2022

24390176R00104